Literacy in development: a series of training monographs

Other titles in *Literacy in development: a series of training monographs,* Series editor, H. S. Bhola, Professor of Education, Indiana University at Bloomington, Indiana, United States of America:

The use of radio in adult literacy education, by Richard C. Burke

Learning to read and reading to learn: an approach to a system of literacy instruction, by Sohan Singh

Understanding visual literacy and communication, by Anne C. Zimmer and Fred A. Zimmer

The ABCs of literacy: lessons from linguistics, by Kenneth L. Baucom

Evaluating functional literacy, by H. S. Bhola

Towards scientific literacy, by Frederick J. Thomas and Allan K. Kondo

Literacy in development: a series of training monographs
Series editor: H. S. Bhola, Indiana University

Programmed instruction for literacy workers

*A guide for developing self-instructional materials
and strategies for adult learners,
literacy teachers and discussion leaders.*

Sivasailam Thiagarajan
*Instructional Developer,
University of Mid America,
Lincoln, Nebraska (United States of America)*

Hulton Educational Publications Ltd.,
in co-operation with the
International Institute for Adult Literacy Methods
Tehran   1976

Acknowledgements

The IIALM acknowledges its gratitude to the Series Editor, Prof. H. S. Bhola of Indiana University, and to the authors whose efforts he has enlisted. Appreciation is also expressed to the German Foundation for International Development and the German Adult Education Association for organizing a meeting of literacy specialists to review this and other monographs in the series. Special thanks are owed to Dr. Gerhard Fritz and Mrs. Brigitte Frehy, Directors General of the German Foundation for International Development, and to Dr. Josef Muller of the Foundation's Science and Education Branch.

The cover design for the series is by Mr. Fred Zimmer. Mr. David Kahler of the IIALM has served as project co-ordinator for the monograph series. Spanish editions of the monographs are being published by the Editorial Magisterio Español, S.A., for the Oficina de Educación Iberoamericana for whose co-operation thanks are expressed to the Secretary General of the OEI, H.E. Rodolfo Barón Castro. Arrangements for translations into other languages are under discussion.

Lastly, and above all, gratitude is expressed to the Government of Iran for a special grant which has made the series possible. In particular, appreciation is due to H.E. Mr. Safi Asfia, Minister of State and Chairman of the IIALM's Governing Board; H.E. Dr. Abdol Hossein Sami'i, Minister of Science and Higher Education and to Mr. Fereidoun Ardalan, Secretary General of the Iranian National Commission for Unesco.

The International Institute for Adult Literacy Methods was established in 1968 under an agreement between Unesco and the Government of Iran. Its functions are to provide documentation, research and training services on methods, media, materials and techniques of adult literacy. The IIALM operates a documentation service and publishes three journals: *Literacy Discussion* and *Literacy Work* appear quarterly; *Literacy Documentation* is published three times annually. A Governing Board composed of representatives of Unesco and the Governments of Iran and Pakistan oversees the programme of the Institute.

Published in 1976 by Hulton Educational Publications Ltd., Raans Road, Amersham, Bucks., England in co-operation with the International Institute for Adult Literacy Methods, P.O. Box 1555, Tehran, Iran.

Printed in Great Britain by John Gardner (Printers) Ltd.

Invitation to the reader

Reading a book can be like conversing with a knowledgeable friend. However, even the most well-written book is a one way conversation. The author speaks and the reader listens. Sometimes the author anticipates the reader's thoughts and questions. Otherwise, the questions remain unanswered.

The International Institute for Adult Literacy Methods (IIALM) wishes to assist the reader of this monograph (and other monographs in this series) to engage in a genuine dialogue. We live today in a world where communications between most parts of the globe are reasonably fast, most often dependable and not too expensive. We suggest that the reader send his questions to the IIALM—general and specific—as well as his problems in working with these materials. The Institute would be glad to help or to put the reader in touch with someone who can.

The reader should let the Institute know if, in his judgment, this monograph has succeeded in doing what it started out to do: (a) to introduce the reader to the programmed instruction technique; (b) to indicate the various possibilities in the use of programmed instruction in adult literacy work; and (c) to provide sufficient guidelines to the reader to enable him to *do something practical* with the monograph in his working life. IIALM would like to hear of any suggestions the reader may have about improvements to subsequent editions of this monograph.

Translation of books that are programmed and of books that include illustrations of programmed instruction presents special problems. Again, IIALM would be glad to be of assistance in the solution of these problems.

With the readers' help, IIALM can indeed become a significant institution, an international correspondence college of literacy. There is the need. The address to write to is:

Dr. John W. Ryan, Director,
International Institute for Adult
    Literacy Methods,
P.O. Box 1555,
Tehran, Iran.

Editor's preface

This series of technical monographs on *Literacy in development* has a definite practical intent. The intent is to bring to literacy workers in Asia, Africa, Latin America and elsewhere good technical help in their day-to-day work.

We are keenly and painfully aware of the questions that can be asked in honesty or in anger: Does it really make sense to talk of literacy in a world crowded with the hungry? Do we have our priorities right?

Words alone, of course, would not be enough. Words, whether written to be read, or bounced off satellites to be broadcast, would be mere words unless institutional changes also occur. Existing social, economic and political arrangements will have to be redesigned if our social aspirations are to be fulfilled.

Yet words must be written to be read, or spoken to be heard, for the new social visions to be shared, for the new technologies to gain diffusion, and for new norms and values to be widely internalized. The road to desirable futures seems to go through 'Media Avenue' or better perhaps through 'Literacy Lane'. The hope is that literacy, by making adult men and women literate, would make them independent participants in their symbolic environments. We can thus find a direct and generative connection between literacy and development, between the literacy primer and the ploughshare.

Literacy workers, unfortunately, have not had the benefit of much professional help from universities or teachers' colleges either in the developed or the developing world. Often literacy organizers have trained their own workers, and written their own materials. They have kept their experience to themselves, for there has been no way of sharing it across projects even within the same regions.

The International Institute for Adult Literacy Methods in Tehran seeks to provide the professional and technical help that has been unavailable to literacy workers around the world. The Institute has been instrumental already in producing an impressive body of literature on literacy for use by literacy workers. The present series of technical monographs on *Literacy in development* is one more step in the same direction.

Through this series we will bring to literacy workers useful insights from the social and behavioural sciences—sociology, psychology, political science, anthropology, communication, linguistics and pedagogy—that would illuminate their problems and offer possible solutions. We will talk directly to the concerns of literacy organizers and workers. For example, we will deal with questions of planning and administration of literacy projects, production of literacy primers and follow-up reading materials, media use in literacy work and evaluation of literacy programmes. At the front of this book we have included a list of titles of monographs in this series. More titles will be added in the future. The monographs will be simply written and will be well illustrated.

This particular monograph deals with a teaching-learning technique called 'programmed instruction'. Programmed instruction is both a *process* and a *product*. As a *process,* programmed instruction is a systematic approach to teaching. It involves learner analysis: What does the learner know already? It involves task analysis: What tasks will the learner learn? In other words, what are the learning objectives? Finally, it involves evaluation of the teaching-learning strategies and materials to make the needed modifications in both.

Programmed instruction as *product* is a specially written book or a total package of books, filmstrips, laboratory experiences, tests, etc. It is self-instructional. The programmed instruction material is self-instructional because it uses highly structured sequencing, small steps in presenting content, is self-paced by the learner while providing him with knowledge of results and, therefore, reinforcements, as he engages in the learning tasks.

The usefulness of programmed materials in literacy work should perhaps begin to become apparent. Adult men and women, once they are semi-literate, can be helped to become independent learners. They can take programmed materials in reading, arithmetic, health and hygiene, child care, poultry farming and pest control home to work with. This should be an important consideration for literacy workers who seldom work with adults in class groups for more than four to six months.

While programmed instruction is excellent for independent study, programmed materials can be used in group situations as well. Indeed, in countries where literacy teachers themselves are not too well prepared to teach, programmed tutorial systems can be developed which would assure a certain level of performance by teachers. The role of programmed instruction in the in-service training of literacy teachers, and in staff development of all others working on literacy projects, can be truly significant.

Why a special monograph on *Programmed instruction for literacy workers?* There has been indeed enough written on programmed instruction. But there is hardly a book that deals directly with the world of the literacy worker and talks specifically to his concerns. This monograph not only brings in one place all of the most important ideas on programmed instruction, but also shows how those ideas could be put to work by literacy workers.

Most educators agree that programmed instruction as a process has made much more significant contributions to teaching and learning than has programmed instruction as product. In other words, the focus on the learner, the systematic progression from learning objectives to tasks in sequencing and structuring of teaching content, and the testing of materials for improvement have been very influential ideas. These ideas have made much greater impact on education than actual instructional materials produced in programmed format. Thus, even if literacy workers who read this monograph never write a programmed book, they would still have learned significantly from the monograph about the process of teaching and learning and about designing instructional and developmental strategies.

The preceding should not be taken as a suggestion to stop with the process and forget about the product. Programmed instruction materials should be developed. Literacy teachers, supervisors, and extension workers collaborating with literacy workers on functional literacy projects should attempt small programmed sequences on various topics of instruction and extension. They should develop teachers' newsletters in programmed format for their literacy teachers who cannot be brought together too often for in-service training. My own experience with developing programmed materials at Literacy House, Lucknow (India), some years ago has left me with the strong conviction that programmed instruction has great possibilities in adult literacy. Let us pioneer.

H.S. Bhola

Contents

CHAPTER ONE

What is programmed instruction?

This book is about programmed instruction. The word 'programmed' has two meanings: (a) the instructional material is carefully organized; and (b) the planning and preparation of the instructional material is systematic. In this chapter examples of the systematic process of programmed instruction will be explained. I will also give you an example of the organized instructional material which is called a 'programmed instructional unit' or a 'programme'. Giving a real example in a 'strange' language on a 'strange' subject will not be useful to you. Therefore, I shall use an imaginary example in English. By doing this, I can illustrate many of the important aspects of programmed instruction. However, you have to translate this example to your own culture and language to make it more meaningful.

Figure 1 is from a programme on 'thakali' plants. The programme is divided into a number of short sections called 'frames' each of which will be printed on a separate page in the actual programme. This example comes from the middle of the programme when the learner has already completed the first twenty frames. The programme attempts to teach three things: (a) to transplant thakali plants using the proper procedure; (b) to read and follow simple directions in order to answer different types of questions; and (c) to write some of the functional words correctly.

All the frames in this sample programme have a number of common characteristics:

1. *Frames give new information.* All frames except the last one are called 'teaching frames' because each frame in this sequence gives the learner some new information. Frame 21, for example, gives information about the appearance of a thakali plant. In Frame 22 new information is given by a picture. The last frame does not give any new information,

FIGURE 1. *An example of programmed instruction*

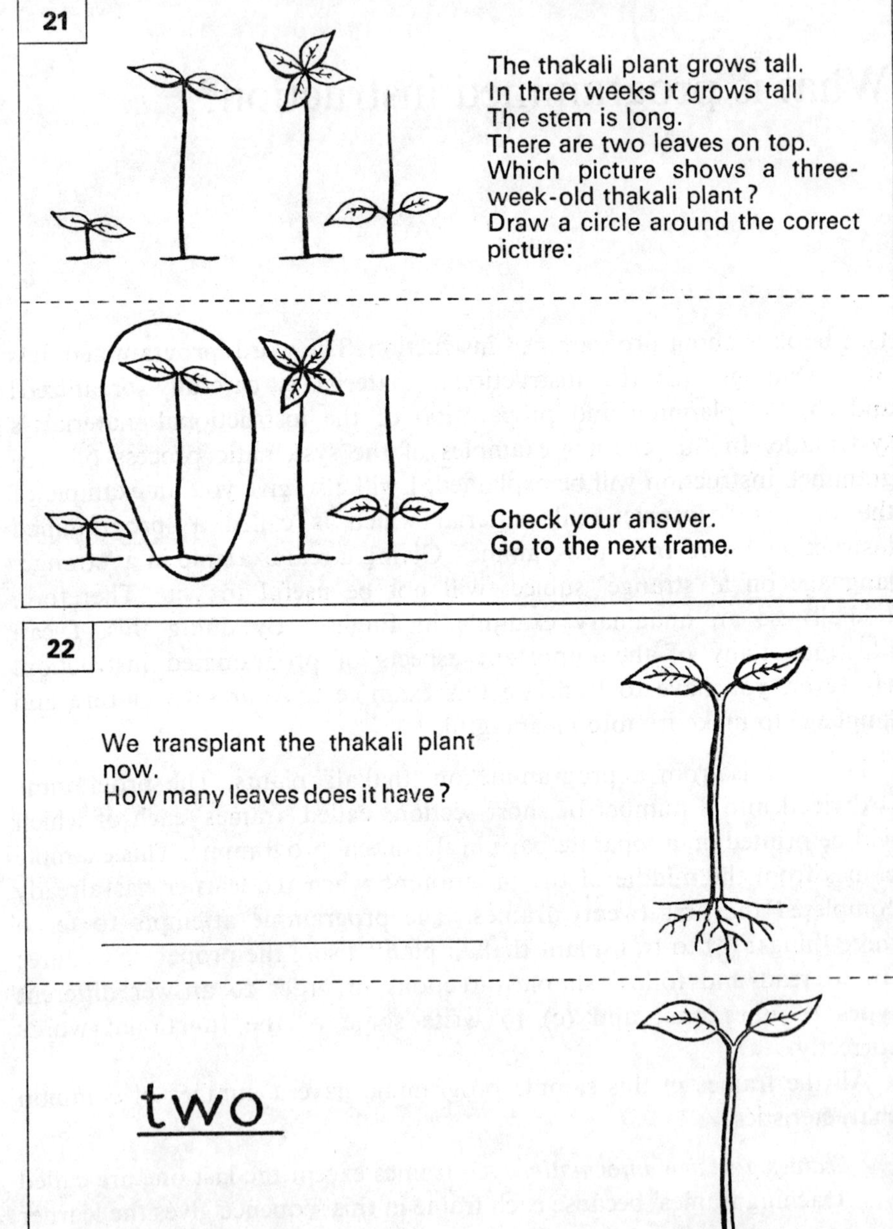

23

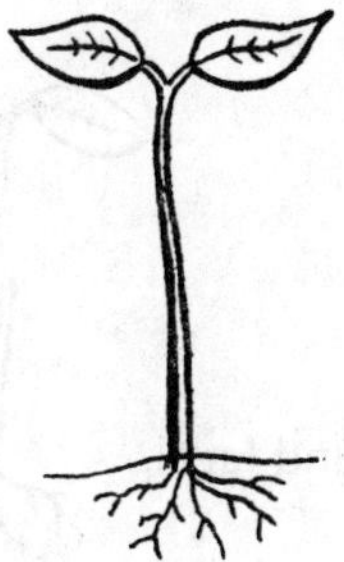

We dig up the thakali plant.
This thakali is three weeks old.
It has a long stem and two leaves.
We are going to trans________this
thakali.

---

trans **plant**

Check your answer.

Go to the next frame.

24

This is how we transplant the
thakali.

The root is under the ground.
Is most of the stem under the ground also? ________

Yes

Check your answer.
Go to the next frame.

25

We transplant the thakali.
We bury the root under ground.
We bury most of the stem under
the ground.
Draw a line in this picture to show the ground level.

- -

Check your answer.
Go to the next frame.

(See Frame 26 on next page.)

but asks a question about the previous frames. This type of frame is called a 'test frame'.

2. *Frames ask a question.* Each frame in the sample asks a question. The type of question varies from one frame to the next. For example, the question in Frame 21 asks the student to 'select' the answer by drawing a circle around one of the pictures. Frame 22 asks the student to 'write' his answer. Frame 26 asks the student to 'match' words and pictures. All these questions ask the student to show his understanding of the information given in that frame or in the previous frames.

3. *Frames give the correct answer.* In the sample frames, the correct answer is given below the broken line. The student can use this to check his own answer. In some programmes the correct answer is placed on the back of the page. This prevents the student from seeing the answer before giving his own answer.

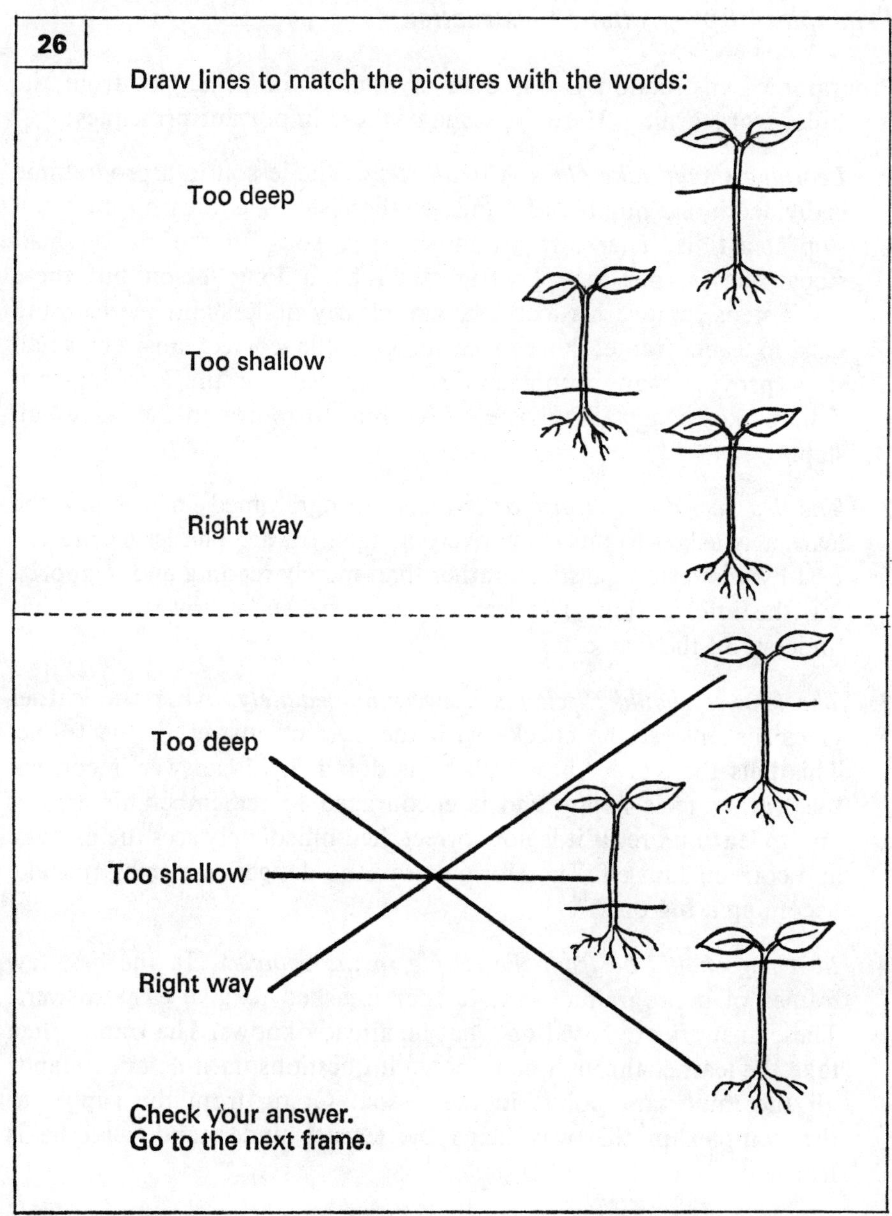

When using the programme the student does these four things repeatedly: (a) reads the new information given in the frame; (b) answers the question in the frame; (c) checks his answer with the correct answer; and (d) goes to the next frame and repeats the steps.

Principles of programmed instruction

Programmed instruction is based on a number of principles from the psychology of learning. Here are some of these important principles:

1. *Learning should take place in small steps.* The lesson in a programme is divided into a number of frames so that the student learns one small step at a time. There are a number of reasons for the use of small steps: the learner may be frightened by a long lesson but these small steps remove his fears; he can clearly understand the learning task in each frame; he can easily give the correct answer; small steps provide many opportunities for success for the learner; even if he makes a mistake, it is easy for him to return to the last small step.

2. *The learner should learn actively.* In programmed instruction the learner is asked to answer actively in each frame. The learner learns best by answering questions rather than merely reading and memorizing the information. The learner's answers show how well he has understood the frame.

3. *The learner should check his answers immediately.* After the learner gives his answer, he checks with the correct answer in the frame. This tells the learner how well he is doing. If his answer is correct, the learner feels happy and is encouraged to remember his answer and to learn more. If it is not correct, he immediately sees the mistake and corrects himself. Therefore, there is no danger of a small mistake becoming a big one.

4. *Learning should be from the simple to the complex.* In the first few frames of a programme, the learner is asked to give easy answers. These answers are based on what he already knows. The frames then take the learner through more difficult questions until he understands all the important points in the lesson. Going from the simple to the complex in this way helps the learner understand what he is learning.

5. *The learner should learn at his own speed.* In a classroom, some learners find the lesson too fast and others find it too slow. In a programme the learner can go fast if he finds the frames easy or slow down if he finds them difficult. He can also make up his own timetable for learning from the programme. He can study at any time of day or night.

The programming process

Let us now discuss the procedure by which the programme on the thakali plant was prepared. This procedure is called the programming process and it is shown in Figure 2. As you can see, there are three stages in the programming process: analysis; writing; and revision. Each of these stages is divided into a number of steps.

FIGURE 2. *The programming process*

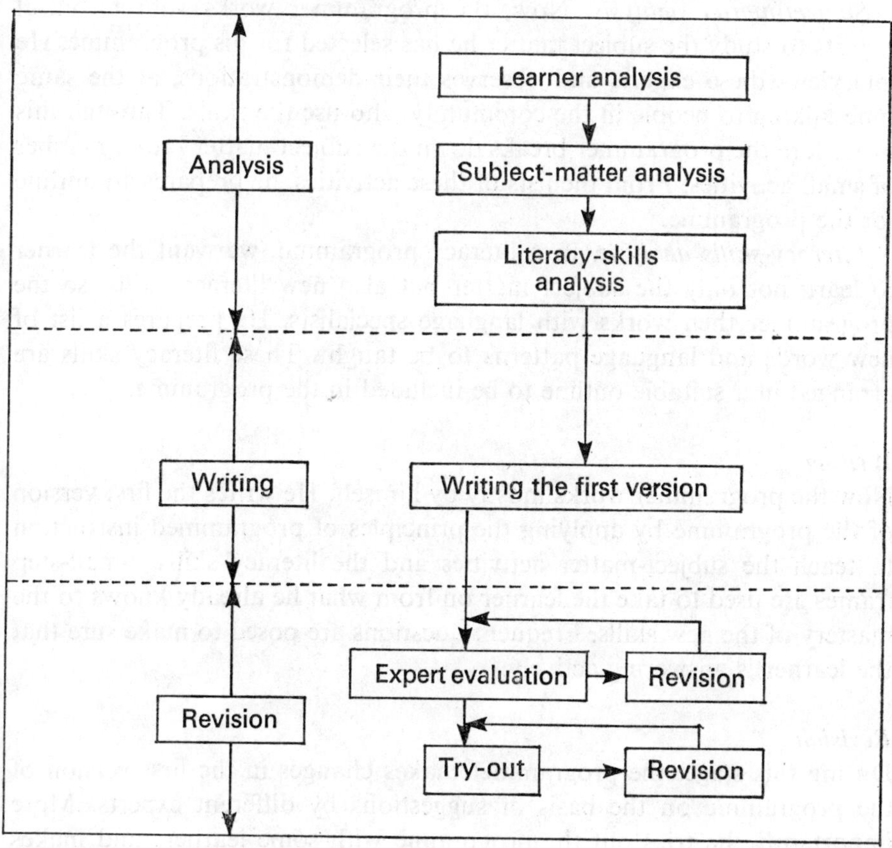

Analysis

During this stage the programmer (the person who prepares the programme) produces an outline. He does this by studying the needs of the learner, the structure of the subject matter and the requirements of the language. Here are brief descriptions of the three steps in the analysis stage:

Learner analysis. In this step the programmer works with other literacy workers, members of the community and his learners. He begins by deciding to which community his learners belong. This community may be described narrowly (e.g., 'members of the co-operative society in the Sidi Saad region') or broadly (e.g., 'cotton farmers'). Having described the community, the programmer next selects a subject matter which is useful to this community. After this, the programmer finds out how much his learners already know about this subject. He also finds out what literacy skills they already have.

Subject-matter analysis. Now, the programmer works with technical experts to study the subject matter he has selected for his programme. He interviews these experts and observes their demonstrations, at the same time talking to people in the community who use the skills. Through this procedure the programmer breaks down the subject matter into a number of small activities. From the lists of these activities, he prepares an outline for the programme.

Literacy-skills analysis. In a literacy programme, we want the learner to learn not only the subject matter but also new literacy skills, so the programmer then works with language specialists. He prepares a list of new words and language patterns to be taught. These literacy skills are arranged in a suitable outline to be included in the programme.

Writing

Now the programmer works mostly by himself. He writes the first version of the programme by applying the principles of programmed instruction to teach the subject-matter activities and the literacy skills. Small-step frames are used to take the learner on from what he already knows to the mastery of the new skills. Frequent questions are posed to make sure that the learner is answering actively.

Revision

During this stage, the programmer makes changes in the first version of the programme on the basis of suggestions by different experts. More importantly, he tries out the programme with some learners and makes changes on the basis of their answers and comments. The two steps in this stage are briefly described below.

Expert evaluation. The programmer asks for suggestions from different experts to improve his first version. These experts may give suggestions for adding more information in the frames, changing the types of questions, giving more suitable examples and rearranging the sequence.

Try-outs. One of the important principles of programmed instruction is that the best judge of a programme is the learner. Here, the programmer tries out the programme on an adult learner. The purpose of this step is not to test the learner, but to find out how the programme can be improved. At first, the programmer tries out his programme on single learners and makes suitable changes on the basis of the mistakes they make. Then he collects more information from groups of learners and makes additional changes.

As you can see from Figure 2, the arrows going back from the expert evaluation and try-out steps signify a number of changes made in the programme. The expert evaluation step is repeated until the experts and the programmer are satisfied with the revisions. Similarly, the try-out step is repeated until new learners show effective results.

Resources needed for the programming process

People

As you can see from the 'Who' column of Table 1, the programming process is not a single-handed job. If there is enough money, we may employ different experts and programmers. Unfortunately, literacy work is usually undertaken on a small budget. You may have to depend entirely on the local resources and volunteers, although you can serve different functions in the programming process by learning different skills. However, there is one person whom you can never replace—the learner, who is the most important one in the analysis, writing and revision of the programme.

Skills

As shown in the 'How' column of Table 1, the programming process requires you to have many different skills. We hope that this book will help you to learn some of these skills. Of course, you do not become an expert programmer merely by reading books. It is important that you, too, learn actively. As you study this book we would like you to prepare a short programme on any topic you like. At the end of each chapter of this book we have given you a practical exercise to make sure that you are using what you have learned.

Time

You will not be able to write a programme in a couple of days. Preparing a programme takes a lot of time. Because of this, you will have to be sure

TABLE 1. *Resources needed for the programming process*

WHAT?	WHO?	HOW?	WHY?	HOW MUCH TIME?
Learner analysis	Programmer, community leaders, literacy workers and other members of the community	Interviews and discussions	To produce a description of the community and what its members already know	
Subject-matter analysis	Programmer, experts and people in the community	Demonstrations by experts. Interviews and observation by the programmer	To divide the subject matter into a number of learning activities and to prepare a suitable sequence for the programme	
Literacy-skills analysis	Programmer, language teachers and linguists	Interviews and discussions	To prepare lists of words, sentence patterns, and other elements of language to be taught by the programme	
Writing	Programmer	Using the principles of programmed instruction to write the programme	To produce the first version of the programme	
Expert evaluation	Programmer and technical and language experts	Revising the programme on the basis of the suggestions from the experts	To produce an edited version of the programme	
Try-out	Programmer and learners from the community	Trying out the programme with single learners and groups. Revising the programme on the basis of the information collected during the try-out	To produce an improved version of the programme	

that you have chosen important subject matter and literacy skills. The production of a programme may take any time from a month to a year, depending upon its length and the resources you have. We have left the last column of Table 1 blank so that you can make your own time estimates.

Summary

In this chapter we have discussed the important characteristics of a programme, the principles of programmed instruction and the programming process. A programme is divided into a number of small frames. Teaching frames present new information, ask a question about it and give the correct answer. Test frames ask a question about the previous teaching frames. In using a programme, the learner reads the information given in the frame, answers the question and checks his answer. He repeats these steps with each frame of the programme.

The important principles of programmed instruction are as follows: (a) learning should take place in small steps; (b) the learner should learn actively by answering questions frequently; (c) the learner should check his answers immediately; (d) learning should be from the simple to the complex; (e) the learner should learn at his own speed.

The programming process is the systematic procedure by which a programme is planned and prepared. There are a number of steps in this process, each of which is illustrated in Table 1.

PRACTICAL EXERCISE

The remaining chapters of this book will give you more details of each step of the programming process. This will be a good time for you to think about the programme you are going to prepare in general terms. Study Table 1 carefully and answer the following questions:

1. *Who will be the learners for your programme? Briefly describe the community to which your learners belong.*

....

....

2. *What will be the subject matter for your programme?*

....

....

3. *Who are the 'experts', friends and future learners who can help you during the programming process? Write down their names.*

....

....

4. *How long will it take you to prepare the complete programme? Estimate the number of days required for each step of the programming process and write it down in the last column of Table 1.*

CHAPTER TWO

Who are you going to teach?

Learner analysis

Learner analysis is the first step in the preparation of a programme. We begin this step by describing the community to which our learners belong. We then collect information on different needs of this community. Then, we find out what the learners already know.

Why undertake learner analysis?

A clear description of our learners helps us prepare an effective programme for them. The information collected about the learners helps us in the following specific ways:

1. Through a study of the problems facing the learners we identify a suitable subject matter for our programme. Learners using the programme immediately see its usefulness. This increases the interest level of the programme.
2. We find out a number of common experiences related to the subject matter. This enables us to provide meaningful examples in our programme. These examples make the programme more interesting and useful.
3. Finding out what the learners already know about the subject helps us avoid making the programme too easy or too hard. This information permits us to build upon what the learners already know.
4. Finding out the language level of the learners enables us to plan the literacy objectives for the programme. Once again, we can begin at the learners' level and gradually improve their literacy skills.
5. Learner analysis is related to the next step of subject-matter analysis. Learner analysis provides the general topic for the programme and subject-matter analysis divides it into smaller units.

Learners and experts

In learner analysis, we use many sources of information from both within and outside the community of learners. The best way to identify the characteristics of the learners is by directly observing and interviewing them. However, outside experts (e.g., agricultural, governmental and medical officers living in the community) can provide us with some special information not available from the learners because they may not realize their own weaknesses, prejudices and problems. Also, our learners may be ashamed of their 'ignorance' and it may not be a good idea to ask direct questions about things they do not know.

The three phases of learner analysis

In the first phase of learner analysis, we clearly describe the community to which our learners belong. In the second phase, we select a suitable subject matter for the programme based on the needs of this community. In the third phase, we find out what our learners already know. Here are some specific things you should do in each of these phases:

(a) *Describe the community to which our learners belong*

1. In consultation with other experts, select the future learners for the literacy programme. Describe the community in such specific terms as 'citrus farmers in the Sidi Saad Region'.

(b) *Select a suitable subject matter for programming*

2. Discuss, with different experts, the economic and social developmental goals for the community.

3. Study different surveys, records, reports and other documents to understand the needs of the community.

4. Interview the experts about the needs of the community.

5. Interview leaders of the community about their needs.

6. Interview and observe people in the community and make a final selection of an urgent need.

7. Select a subject matter which will help the community deal with this need.

8. Check back with the experts, local leaders and learners to see if they agree that the selected subject is important.

(c) *Find out what the learners already know*

9. Identify different skills related to the selected subject matter.

10. Make up a set of questions to collect information on what the learners already know.

11. Interview experts for their estimate of what the learners already know.

12. Interview and observe learners to get a clearer picture of what they already know.

Practical suggestions

How to describe the community to which the learners belong

This first phase is a very important one. All future activities in the programming process are determined by the way in which your learners are described. We may define our learner community in terms of a region (e.g., 'people living in the Ghab region'), in terms of what they already know (e.g., 'neo-literates who have completed the primer'), or in terms of other characteristics (e.g., 'married men with more than three children'). A very specific group such as 'married men with more than three children who have successfully completed the primary literacy class' will help us to prepare a very effective programme. However, the use of this programme will be limited to a small group. On the other hand, a very broad group such as 'all farmers in different regions of the country cultivating different crops' provides us with a larger community, but it is very doubtful if a single programme can serve such a big group.

How to select a suitable subject matter for the programme

In this phase of learner analysis we select a suitable subject matter which fulfils an important need of the community. This procedure begins with outside sources of information and moves to the inner circle of learners as shown in Figure 3.

We begin by making up a questionnaire which is used with the experts in the field. A sample questionnaire is shown as Figure 4. A direct question to an expert about the needs of the community will result in a special opinion. A medical officer, for example, would look at the community from one point of view and an agricultural expert from another. In order to make their opinions more objective, we interview each expert by asking for his list of major developmental goals for the region. Then we ask the expert for a list of problems which stand in the way of reaching these goals. Examples of such problems include reduced harvests, increased accidents in a factory, sick children and community members being cheated by fraudulent tax collectors. The problem is the gap between what we want to happen (e.g., 10 per cent increase in cotton production) and what is actually happening (5 per cent shortfall). At the end of a number of interviews with experts, you may have collected a large number of problem statements. Your task now is to reduce it to a few problems. You do this first by eliminating those problems which are beyond the control of the community. For example, if the shortfall in cotton production is due to lack of fertilization, it is reasonably within community control. However,

FIGURE 3. *Procedure for selecting a suitable subject matter for the programme*

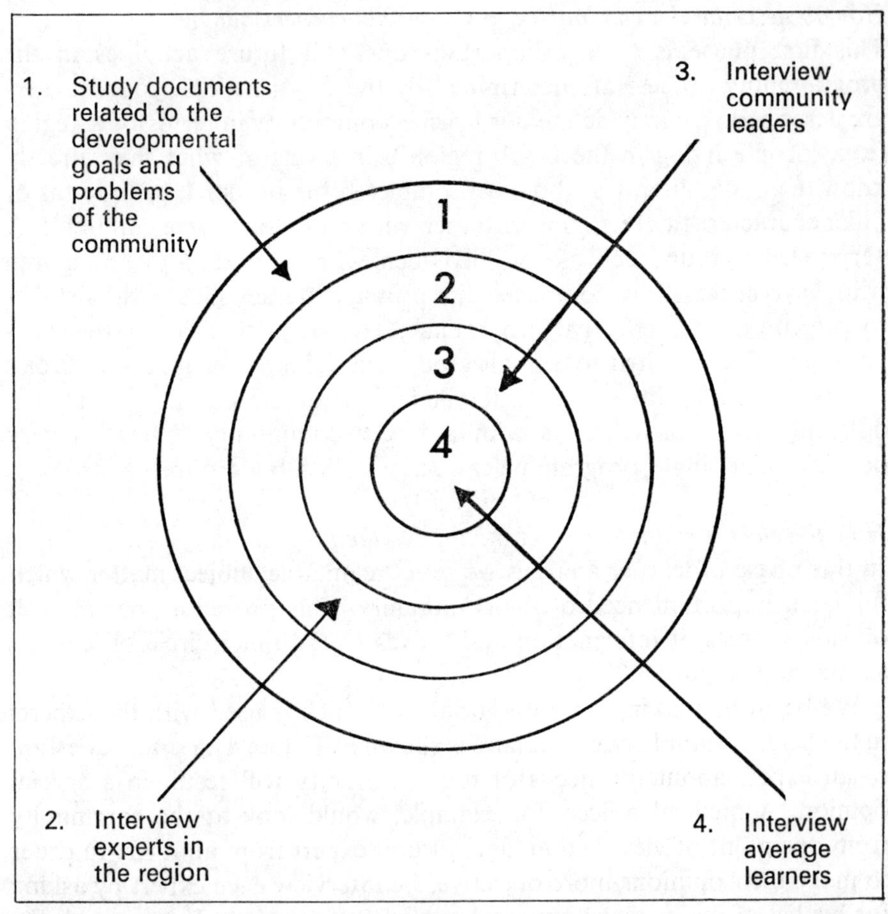

if it is due to a drought in the region, obviously there is very little the community can do about it.

Our next task is to guess the reason for each problem. In general, this reason may be due to: (a) lack of resources; (b) lack of motivation; or (c) lack of skills and knowledge. Not all problems suggest suitable subject matter for a programme. If there is no fertilizer available in the region, teaching cotton growers how to use fertilizer is useless. Similarly, if farmers do not believe in the use of fertilizer, teaching them how to use fertilizer without first changing their attitude is also useless. An ideal situation for a programme exists if farmers have a generous supply of fertilizers and believe in its effectiveness but do not know the proper procedure for using it.

FIGURE 4. *Need-selection questionnaire*

<table>
<tr><td colspan="3" align="center">NEED-SELECTION QUESTIONNAIRE</td></tr>
<tr><td colspan="3">1. What are the major developmental goals of the community?</td></tr>
<tr><td colspan="3">..</td></tr>
<tr><td colspan="3">..</td></tr>
<tr><td colspan="3">2. What are some of the problems in reaching these goals?</td></tr>
<tr><td colspan="3">..</td></tr>
<tr><td colspan="3">..</td></tr>
<tr><td colspan="3">3. Which of these problems are beyond the control of the community?</td></tr>
<tr><td colspan="3">..</td></tr>
<tr><td colspan="3">..</td></tr>
<tr><td colspan="3">4. Classify the problems according to the main reason:</td></tr>
<tr><td>Lack of resources</td><td>Lack of motivation</td><td>Lack of skills and knowledge</td></tr>
<tr><td>...................</td><td>...................</td><td>...................</td></tr>
<tr><td>...................</td><td>...................</td><td>...................</td></tr>
<tr><td>...................</td><td>...................</td><td>...................</td></tr>
<tr><td colspan="3">5. List some problems which are caused by a lack of skills and knowledge:</td></tr>
<tr><td colspan="3">..</td></tr>
<tr><td colspan="3">..</td></tr>
</table>

Interviewing members of the community

We are now ready to move into the learners' community itself and interview its leaders and members. We use the same questionnaire (Figure 4) for suggesting the questions for this interview.

The reaction of the community to our interview depends upon a number of factors. Some people feel flattered, while others are frightened about talking to official visitors. Here are some suggestions for conducting effective interviews:

1. Begin by establishing friendly understanding with the person being interviewed. Talk about his family and his job for a few minutes. Explain your purpose and make him realize that he is playing an important role.

2. Do not get into an argument about the importance of literacy. Do not make the learner feel ashamed of his inability to read.

3. Begin with general questions about the person's goals and problems. If your questions appear to be difficult ones, provide him with some examples.

4. If you take notes, wait until an appropriate time and say, 'That's an important idea. Let me write it down'. Use a blank copy of the questionnaire to write down your notes.

5. Encourage the learner to speak freely. Inform him that no one will hear his comments.

6. When the learner has finished with his list of problems, check your list from earlier interviews. Ask him how important he considers each of these problems to be.

7. If the learner agrees with everything you say, force him to make a choice. Ask a question like, 'I agree, all of these are very important to you. But if you were to solve only one of them, which one would you select?'

8. Do not stop the interview suddenly. Summarize the learner's statements and thank him for his courtesy.

After five or six of these interviews, you should have sufficient information for selecting a suitable subject for your programme. You may use the following questions to help you in the final selection of an urgent need in the community:

1. Does the problem prevent the community from reaching its developmental goals?

2. Is the suggested solution simple to teach?

3. Is the solution an effective one? Does it provide dramatic results?

4. Can you teach the solution with a limited vocabulary and controlled language?

5. Are there enough experts in the region to help you during the programming process?

How to find out what the learner already knows

After selecting the subject matter for the programme, we may want to confirm its importance by checking back with the experts and the members of the community. Next, we need to find out the skills and knowledge which have to be taught in order to implement the selected solution. We make up another questionnaire to identify what our learners already know. Figure 5 shows a sample questionnaire.

This questionnaire may be given to the experts to get their estimate of what the learner already knows. As before, we use the questionnaire as an outline for interviews with members of the community. However, some questions have to be removed and others changed. For example, 'What misconceptions do you have?' is a meaningless question. However, a broader question such as 'Tell me everything you know about . . .' will give us useful information.

FIGURE 5. *Sample questionnaire to find out what the learners already know*

QUESTIONNAIRE

Subject matter:
1. What skills and knowledge does the student already possess?
2. What type of professional training does the learner have?
3. What possible misconceptions is the learner likely to have?

Language:
4. How many of the special words does the learner already know?
5. What is the learner's level of reading and writing?
6. What style of language does the learner prefer?

Attitudes:
7. Does the learner understand the need for the subject?
8. Is there an obvious relationship between the problem and the solution?

Learning methods:
9. Is the learner familiar with books and notebooks?
10. Does the learner have any preferences about different types of learning?

PRACTICAL EXERCISE

As you may remember, you have already made some decisions about the programme you are going to prepare. Read your notes about this programme on the last page of Chapter 1. You are now ready to conduct the learner analysis for your programme. Using the suggestions from this chapter, do the following:

1. *Describe the community to which your learners belong.*

....

....

2. *Select a suitable subject matter for your programme based upon the needs of this community.*

....

....

3. *Find out how much your learners already know about the subject matter. Also find out the level of literacy skills of your learners.*

CHAPTER THREE

What subject matter are you going to teach?

This chapter is about subject-matter analysis which gives an outline for the programme. In this chapter, we explain what happens during subject-matter analysis and discuss its importance. We also give you a number of practical suggestions and examples.

Why undertake subject-matter analysis?

Subject-matter analysis provides us with a precise plan for writing the programme. Specifically, this analysis helps us in the following ways:

1. Subject-matter analysis helps us to describe what we want the learner to do after completing the programme. This draws our attention to the learner.

2. In subject-matter analysis we find different learning activities. Since we have already made sure that the subject matter for the programme is suitable to the developmental goals of the community, this procedure guarantees that the programme is directly related to the development of the community. In this way, our programming effort becomes functional and increases the satisfaction of learners.

3. Subject-matter analysis gives us an outline of the programme. It suggests a suitable sequence for beginning at the learner's level and taking him to the mastery of new skills.

4. Subject-matter analysis gives us a set of objectives for the programme. These objectives can be used by other literacy workers to determine whether the programme is suitable for their needs.

5. Subject-matter analysis helps us construct a final test. This test is used to measure the effectiveness of the programme and to identify weak areas which have to be revised.

General procedure for subject-matter analysis

Here is a list of various steps in subject-matter analysis. Practical suggestions for each step are given later.

1. Translate the selected subject matter into a task for the learner to be able to perform after completing the programme.

2. Divide this task into a set of learning activities.

3. Check to make sure that you have a complete set of learning activities.

4. Arrange the learning activities into an outline for the programme.

5. Construct test items for each of the learning activities.

How to state the main task

We identified a suitable subject matter for the developmental needs of the community during the learner analysis. This subject matter is now changed into a statement of instructional task. For example, if the subject matter was the use of soy beans in cooking, here is an initial statement of the instructional task:

The programme shall discuss the cooking of soy beans as a food supplement.

However, this is a task for the programmer. We want to change it to a task for the learner. So we rewrite it in terms of what we want the learner to do upon completing the programme:

The learner will understand the use of soy beans.

This is better than the previous statement because it deals with what the learner will do. However, it is not very clear because the word 'understand' describes a behaviour which cannot be observed by others. In stating our instructional task, it is important to use an observable behaviour:

The learner will cook soy beans.

In this statement, we have an observable learner behaviour. The statement can be made clearer by including some standards for this behaviour:

The learner will cook soy beans. She will do so in such a way that the finished meal will be tasty.

There are many ways to cook soy beans and we may want to specify the method to be used by the learner:

The learner will use 100 grammes of soy beans and a ceramic pot over a slow fire to cook soy beans. The finished meal should be tasty.

In this example we have illustrated the step-by-step procedure for stating our instructional task in the form of a behavioural objective. These steps are reviewed in Table 2 using another example.

TABLE 2. *Procedure for stating behavioural objective*

STEP	EXAMPLE
1. Identify the subject matter based on a need of the community.	The local property tax system has recently been changed. Many farmers are not ready for the larger taxes. Some tax collectors may use dishonest methods to cheat tax payers. The community—members of a co-operative union—need to learn how to calculate the tax themselves.
2. Write a statement of an observable task you want the learner to perform.	The learner will be able to calculate the property tax.
3. Specify standards for the behaviour.	The learner will be able to calculate quarterly, half-yearly, or annual property tax within five per cent of the exact figure.
4. Specify the conditions under which the learner is to perform.	The learner will be given the area of his farm land in acres and the annual tax rate. He will be able to calculate the quarterly, half-yearly, or annual property tax within five per cent of the exact figure.

Here are three more examples of converting a community need into instructional tasks. All of them include an observable learner behaviour, standards for this behaviour and the conditions under which the behaviour takes place.

1. *Community need:* Green-fly attacks on orange groves damage the trees. Orange farmers need to learn how to prevent large-scale attacks. *Statement of the instructional task:* The farmer will be given different pesticides and spraying equipment. He must use them to kill green-flies without damaging the orange trees.

2. *Community need:* A new elementary school has opened in a slum area. Many of the students do not come to classes, however, and neither the parents nor the teachers like this. Parents do not have the time to meet the teacher to explain their children's absence. They are semi-literate but they need to learn how to write short letters to the teacher. *Statement of the instructional task:* The parent must write a letter to the teacher explaining why his/her child was absent from class. This letter should be brief.

3. *Community need:* The government has started a heavy industrial plant in a rural area and it wants to employ local people. Workers are required to fill out an application form. *Statement of the instructional task:* The worker must correctly fill out the application form given to him.

How to analyse the instructional task

In this step of subject-matter analysis, we repeatedly ask ourselves the question: 'What should the learner be able to do in order to perform the instructional task?' For example, in order to calculate the tax on his land, the learner should use the correct area and the correct tax rate and calculate the amount due. These steps are called learning activities. A learning activity is a smaller part of the instructional task and it can be divided into more elementary activities. For example, calculating the amount of tax involves multiplication by the percentage figure and division by 100. Also, since this calculation involves areas and sums of money, the learner should master the activities of converting from one unit into another. We continue this analysis by taking each learning activity and asking 'What should the learner be able to do . . .?' and identifying simpler activities. Farther along in our analysis, we find that multiplication requires the simpler activity of addition which in turn requires the ability to read numerals. Obviously, this type of analysis can go on for a long time. However, we stop the analysis when we reach what the learners already know. With a totally illiterate population, we may continue our analysis to the activity of counting. With learners at secondary school level, our analysis would end sooner.

The nature and the number of learning activities depend upon the behaviours, standards and conditions for the instructional task. Taking the same subject matter of land taxes, let us make it simpler by changing the conditions. Here is the new instructional task:

> Given a table of land taxes, the tax rate on his land and its acreage, the farmer will be able to find out his quarterly, half-yearly or annual tax using the figure for the nearest five-acre area.

Study the tax table in Table 3 for a minute and calculate the tax for an imaginary farmland. Obviously, if someone has to find the 5 per cent tax on a thirty-seven-acre farm for six months, he has to locate the figure at the intersection of the thirty-five-acre row and the 5 per cent column in the middle (half-yearly) section of the table. This helps us find out the learning activity at the first level:

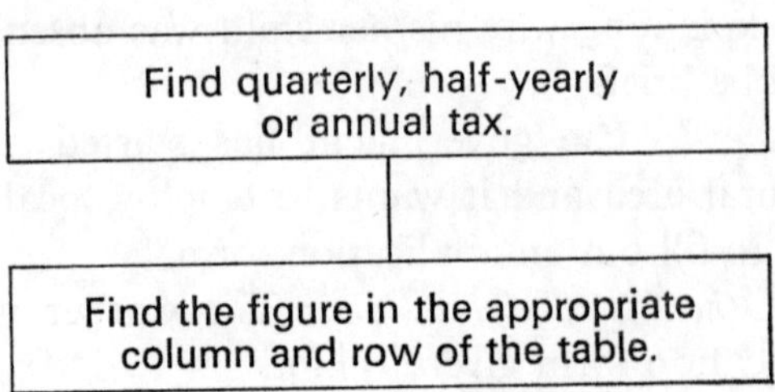

TABLE 3. *Tax tables for use in the sample task analysis*

AREA OF LAND IN ACRES	QUARTERLY TAX TAX RATE				HALF-YEARLY TAX TAX RATE				ANNUAL TAX TAX RATE			
	5%	$6\frac{1}{4}$%	$7\frac{1}{2}$%	10%	5%	$6\frac{1}{4}$%	$7\frac{1}{2}$%	10%	5%	$6\frac{1}{4}$%	$7\frac{1}{2}$%	10%
5	6.00	7.50	9.00	12.00	12.00	15.00	18.00	24.00	24.00	30.00	36.00	48.00
10	12.00	15.00	18.00	24.00	24.00	30.00	36.00	48.00	48.00	60.00	72.00	96.00
15	18.00	22.50	27.00	36.00	36.00	45.00	54.00	72.00	72.00	90.00	108.00	144.00
20	24.00	30.00	36.00	48.00	48.00	60.00	72.00	96.00	96.00	120.00	144.00	192.00
25	30.00	37.50	45.00	60.00	60.00	75.00	90.00	120.00	120.00	150.00	180.00	240.00
30	36.00	45.00	54.00	72.00	72.00	90.00	108.00	144.00	144.00	180.00	216.00	288.00
35	42.00	52.50	63.00	84.00	84.00	105.00	126.00	168.00	168.00	210.00	252.00	336.00
40	48.00	60.00	72.00	96.00	96.00	120.00	144.00	192.00	192.00	240.00	288.00	384.00
45	54.00	67.50	81.00	108.00	108.00	135.00	162.00	216.00	216.00	270.00	324.00	432.00
50	60.00	75.00	90.00	120.00	120.00	150.00	180.00	240.00	240.00	300.00	360.00	480.00

FIGURE 6. *Locating figures in a table*

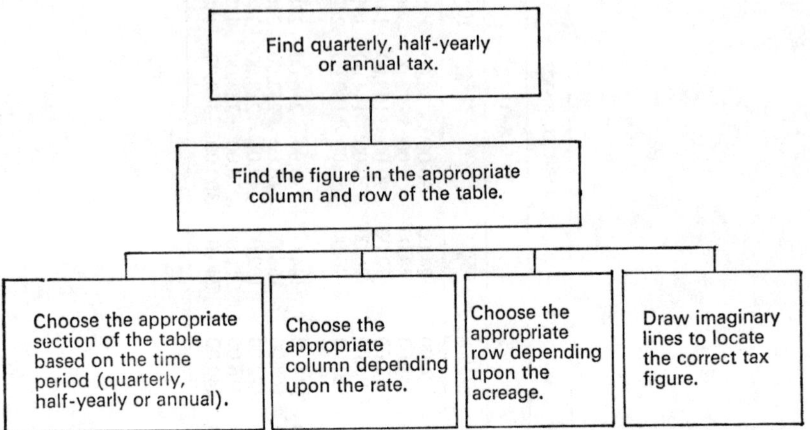

This learning activity can be divided into four simpler ones as shown in Figure 6. The learning activity of choosing the appropriate row requires the simpler activity of being able to round off a figure to the nearest 5. This, in turn, requires some even simpler activities (Figure 7).

FIGURE 7. *Rounding off figures*

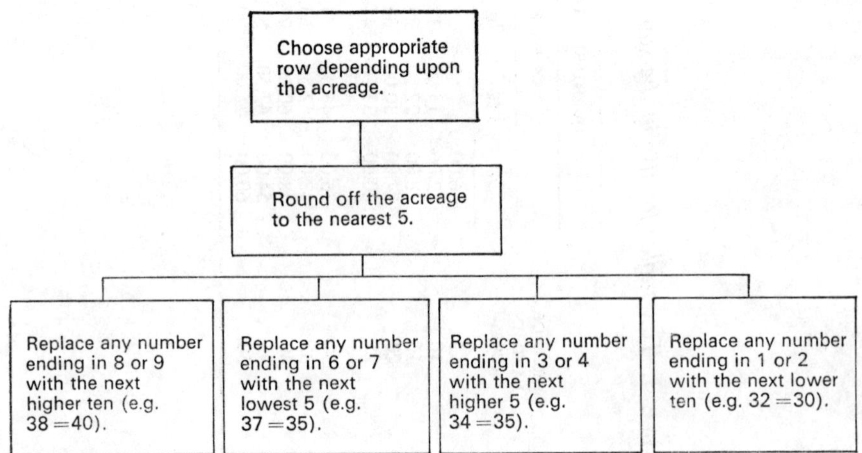

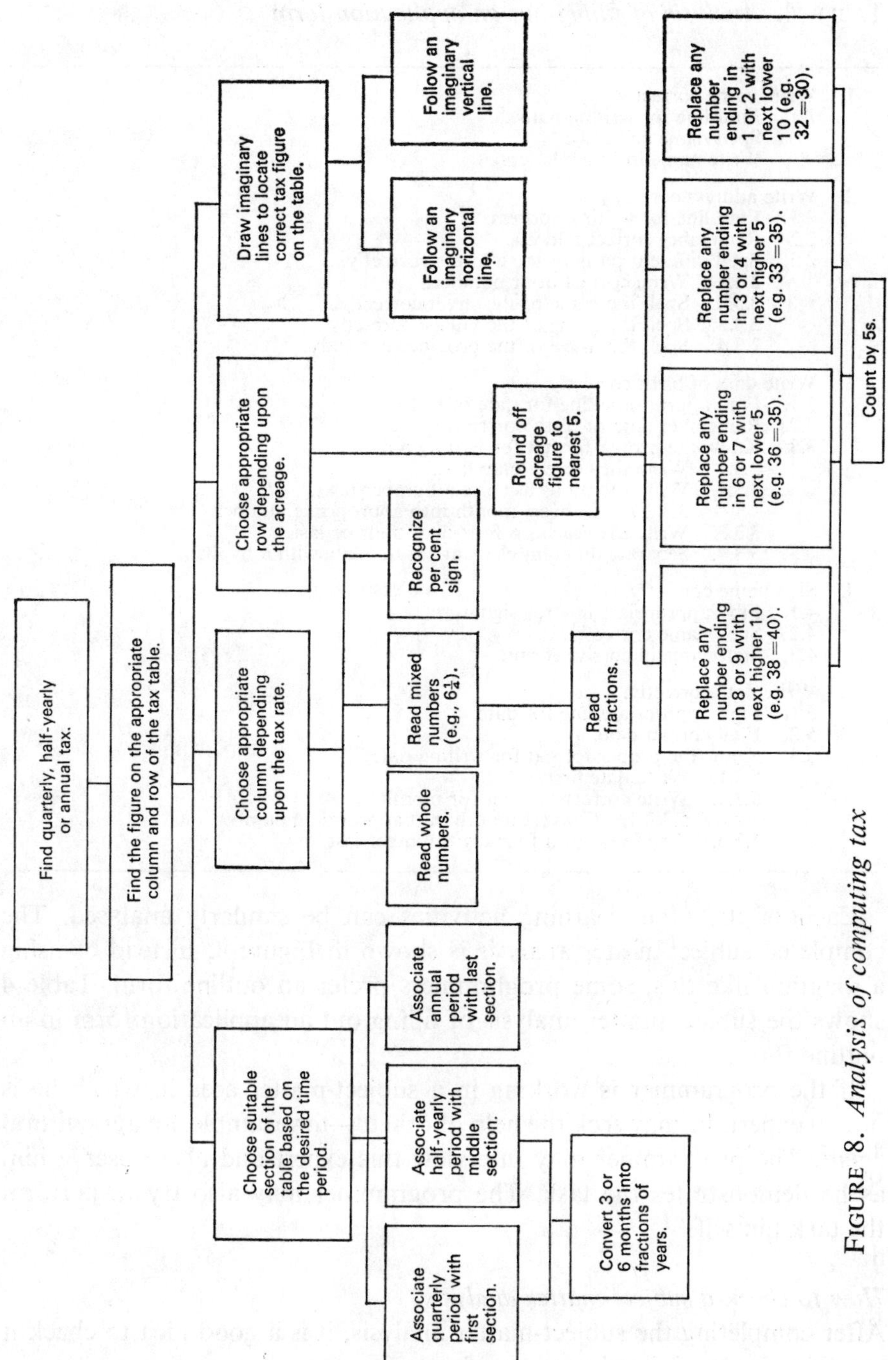

FIGURE 8. *Analysis of computing tax*

TABLE 4. *Analysis of filling out an application form*

---

1. Write name correctly.
   1.1. Find line for writing name.
        Spell name correctly.
        Write name in block letters.

2. Write address correctly.
   2.1. Find line for writing address.
   2.2. Remember correct address.
   2.3. Spell different parts of the address correctly.
        2.3.1. Write correct door number.
        2.3.2. Spell the name of the street correctly.
        2.3.3. Spell the name of the village correctly.
        2.3.4. Spell the name of the province correctly.

3. Write date of birth correctly.
   3.1. Find appropriate line for date of birth.
   3.2. Remember date of birth correctly.
   3.3. Know the proper format for writing a date.
        3.3.1. Write the correct date first.
        3.3.2. Write month as a correct number next.
               3.3.2.1. Convert month into appropriate number.
        3.3.3. Write the year as a four-digit number last.
        3.3.4. Separate different elements of the date with a hyphen.

4. Sign name correctly.
   4.1. Find appropriate line for signature.
   4.2. Spell name correctly.
   4.3. Sign name in cursive script.

5. Write date correctly.
   5.1. Find appropriate line for date.
   5.2. Find correct date.
   5.3. Know the proper format for writing date.
        5.3.1. Write date first.
        5.3.2. Write correct number for month.
               5.3.2.1. Convert month into appropriate number.
        5.3.3. Write year as a four-digit number last.

Each of the other learning activities can be similarly analysed. The completed subject-matter analysis is shown in Figure 8. Instead of using a diagram like this, some programmers prefer an outline form. Table 4 shows the subject-matter analysis of filling out an application form in an outline form.

If the programmer is working in a subject-matter area in which he is not an expert, he may seek the help of others—for example, an agricultural agent. The programmer may interview this expert and also observe him as he demonstrates the task. The programmer may also try to perform the task himself.

How to check a subject-matter analysis
After completing the subject-matter analysis, it is a good idea to check it carefully for the following types of error:

Incomplete analysis. Very often the learning activities may not add up to the instructional task. For example, let us check this analysis to see if the activities add up to the task:

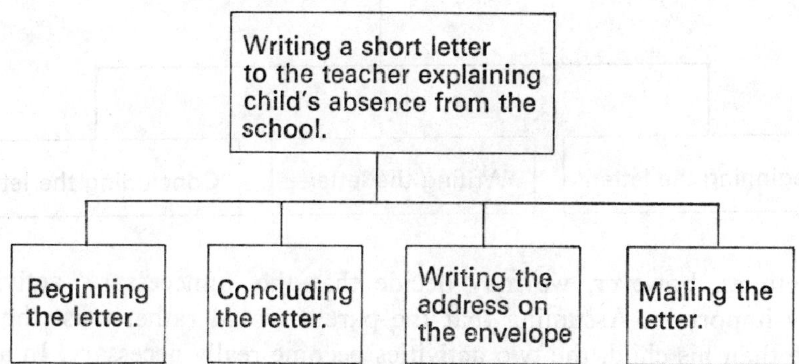

The learning activities talk about the beginning and the end of the letter but not about the letter itself! When you locate a missing activity like this, the correction is simple. Just add this activity in an appropriate location:

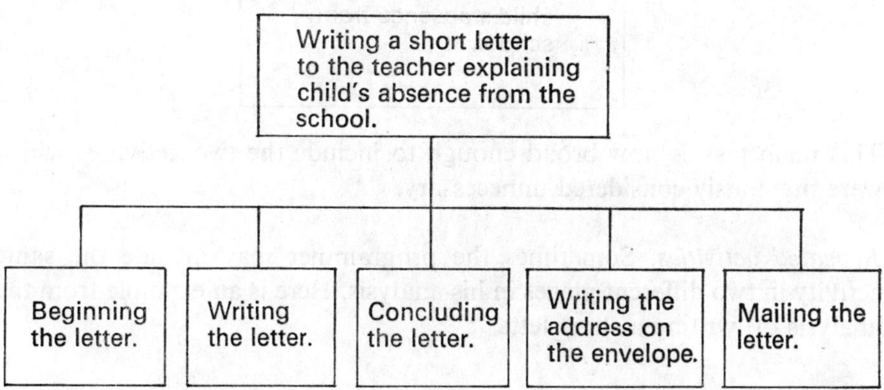

Unnecessary activities. Very often the programmer may analyse the way he teaches a task rather than the task itself. This often results in the listing of unnecessary activities. Looking back at the analysis above, we realize that 'writing the address on the envelope' and 'mailing the letter' have nothing to do with the task of being able to 'write a short letter'.

When we identify an unnecessary activity, there are two different actions we can take. One will be to simply remove it. Assuming that these letters are to be sent through the child to the teacher, we can use this procedure:

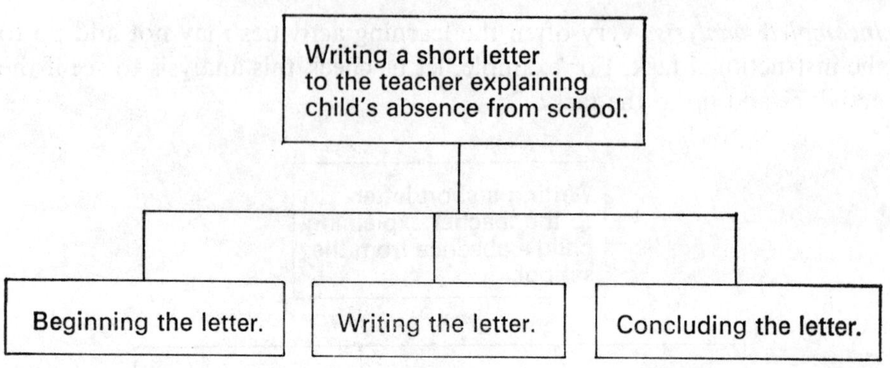

Sometimes, however, we may decide that the 'unnecessary' activity is really important. Assuming that the parent would rather trust the post office than his child, the two activities become really necessary. In a case like this, the correction procedure is to enlarge the main task like this:

Writing and mailing a
short letter to the
teacher explaining
child's absence from
school.

This main task is now broad enough to include the two activities which were previously considered unnecessary.

Repeated activities. Sometimes the programmer may include the same activity in two different places in his analysis. Here is an example from the analysis of 'writing a short letter':

Writing the
teacher's address. Addressing
the envelope.

These two activities are repetitious. The correction procedure in this situation is to eliminate one of them. Table 5 summarizes different types of errors in a subject-matter analysis and what to do about each.

TABLE 5. *Different types of errors in subject-matter analysis*

TYPE OF ERROR	DESCRIPTION OF ERROR	SUITABLE CORRECTION
1. Incomplete analysis.	Different activities do not add up to the task.	Add the missing activity at the appropriate place.
2. Unnecessary activity.	An activity is unnecessary for the performance of the main task.	1. Remove the unnecessary activity or 2. Expand the main task to include this activity.
3. Repeated activity.	The same activity is repeated with minor changes in wording.	Remove one of the activities.

Arranging learning activities in an instructional sequence

Your subject-matter analysis at this stage indicates the interrelationships among various learning activities. Some activities have a logical sequence: 'Writing a short letter', for example, proceeds from the opening, to the main body of the letter, and the closing, in that order. However, the logical sequence may not always be the best teaching sequence. Our learner may already know how to sign his name and this could be a very good starting point for teaching. Generally, sequencing the learning activities involves locating those which the learner already knows and building up from them. A sample instructional sequence is given below in Table 6.

This type of arrangement of learning activities is called an instructional sequence. As you can see, the instructional sequence provides an outline for the programme.

TABLE 6. *Rearrangement into an instructional sequence of the learning activities from Figure 8*

1. Read whole numbers.
2. Read fractions.
3. Read mixed numbers.
4. Read per cent sign.
5. Choose appropriate column depending upon the tax rate.
6. Convert 3 or 6 months into quarterly and half-yearly periods.
7. Associate quarterly period with first section.
8. Associate half-yearly period with middle section.
9. Associate annual period with last section.
10. Choose suitable section of the table based on quarterly, half-yearly or annual time period.
11. Count by 5s.
12. Round off figures to the nearest 5.
13. Select appropriate row on tax table depending upon the acreage.
14. Follow an imaginary vertical line in a table of figures.
15. Follow an imaginary horizontal line in a table of figures.
16. Find the figure on the appropriate column and row of a given table of figures.

How to construct a test

The instructional sequence also permits us to construct a test. Table 7 shows how the instructional sequence from Table 6 is used for preparing such a test. In this procedure, we write a test question for each learning activity. If the learner is unable to find the correct tax amount, it may be due to his failure on any of the simpler activities. By checking him on each activity, we may find out that all he lacks is the ability to choose the correct section of the table. This information permits the literacy teacher to provide the learner with specific remedial instruction.

TABLE 7. *Partial list of test items based on the instructional sequence shown in Table 6*

ACTIVITY	TEST ITEM
1. Read whole numbers	1. Read these numbers: 5, 6, 7, 10.
2. Read fractions.	2. Read these: $\frac{1}{4}$, $\frac{1}{2}$.
3. Read mixed numbers.	3. Read these numbers: $6\frac{1}{4}$, $7\frac{1}{2}$.
4. Read per cent sign.	4. What is this sign called? %
5. Choose appropriate column of the table for a given tax rate.	5. Point to all numbers which go with $7\frac{1}{2}\%$. *(A section of the tax table is shown here.)*
6. Convert 3 or 6 months into quarterly and half-yearly periods.	6. Draw lines to connect two different names for the same period: 3 months half-yearly 6 months quarterly 12 months
......	......
16. Find the figure in the appropriate column and row of a table.	16. What number goes with $6\frac{1}{4}\%$ and 42 acres in this table? *(A section of the tax table is shown here.)*

Summary

Subject-matter analysis begins with the conversion of the community need into a statement of the instructional task in terms of the behaviour of the learner. This task is divided into a set of learning activities. Subject-matter analysis is checked to make sure that it is complete and does not contain any unnecessary or repeated activities. The learning activities are then arranged into a suitable instructional sequence. Test items are written to measure the attainment of each activity in this sequence.

PRACTICAL EXERCISE

Conduct a subject-matter analysis of the topic you selected in the previous exercise. Do the following, using the information from your learner analysis:

1. *Write an instructional task on the basis of the subject matter you selected previously.*
2. *Divide this task into a set of learning activities.*
3. *Check to make sure that the analysis is complete and that it does not contain any unnecessary or repeated learning activities.*
4. *Arrange the learning activities into an instructional sequence.*
5. *Construct test items for each of the learning activities.*

CHAPTER FOUR

What literacy skills are you going to teach?

The learning of the subject matter through a programme is intermixed with the learning of literacy skills. In Chapter 3 we concentrated on the analysis of the subject matter. In this chapter we discuss literacy-skills analysis which involves an analysis of the language to be used in our programme. It also deals with reading, writing and some basic arithmetic skills.

Why undertake literacy-skills analysis?

1. The main reason for undertaking a literacy-skills analysis is that one of the aims of our programme is to teach the skills of reading and writing. While teaching a task gives a special skill to the learner, teaching literacy provides him with a general skill of great value. In the programme we try to teach the learner these literacy skills within the context of a selected subject matter. This makes the learner realize the usefulness of the written language.

2. The type of literacy skills to be taught determines the type of programme. For a community of illiterates, the programme has to be mostly pictures. For semi-literates, it can use a larger vocabulary and more complex sentences. Our literacy-skills analysis enables us to choose the best type.

3. In testing the learner, we have to take into account his language level. It is possible for our learner to know how to perform the task without being able to read and understand the test question. Literacy-skills analysis enables us to make sure that the reading and writing skills required by the test are within the level of what the learner already knows.

4. Literacy-skills analysis enables us to locate words and sentences to be used for teaching the subject matter. It also helps us to identify generative words.

TABLE 8. *Literacy objectives at different levels*

	LITERACY OBJECTIVES		
LEARNER	READING BEHAVIOUR	WRITING BEHAVIOUR	ARITHMETIC BEHAVIOUR
Illiterate	1. Make associations between printed and spoken words. 2. Make associations between printed words and objects. 3. Interpret pictures and use them in the learning of reading skills. 4. Follow oral directions from the teacher.	1. Use writing materials properly. 2. Trace letters.	1. Count 2. Recognize numerals.
Preliterate	1. Sight-read a small number of words. 2. Sound out new words in context. 3. Read words and sentences orally. 4. Demonstrate literal comprehension of what is being read.	1. Copy familiar words. 2. Form and write words in common usage.	1. Perform simple addition. 2. Perform simple subtraction. 3. Use simple fractions.
Neoliterate	1. Sight-read an extensive set of words. 2. Sound out new words in context and in isolation. 3. Read silently and demonstrate comprehension of what is read. 4. Demonstrate ability to understand implied meanings.	1. Form and write words and short sentences in response to specific questions. 2. Write short notes, letters, etc.	1. Perform simple multiplication. 2. Perform simple division.

General procedure for literacy-skills analysis

Here is a list of various steps in the literacy-skills analysis. Practical suggestions for each step are given later.

1. Select a general literacy objective based upon the level of the learner.
2. Select specific objectives for reading, word-attack, and comprehension skills.
3. Record and analyse the language used by learners.

How to select an appropriate literacy objective

Literacy skills for the programme may be elementary or complex depending upon the level of the learner. Thus, for the same main task we may select the sight reading of fifteen words for beginners or the reading of a book for advanced learners. Table 8 lists different literacy objectives for different entry levels, based on similar lists prepared by Dr. William Gray.

How to select specific literacy objectives

After determining the level of the learner, we focus on reading skills suitable at that level. We may consider reading to be an 'instructional task' and perform a 'subject-matter analysis' to identify a set of suitable learning activities:

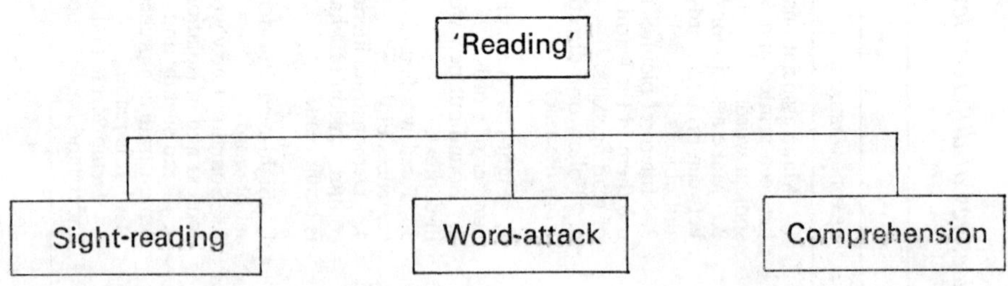

Based on such an analysis by Dr. Douglas Ellson, the task of reading is divided into three activities. 'Sight-reading' is the act of looking at a familiar word and saying it. 'Word-attack' involves sounding out an unfamiliar word by using phonetic elements and context. 'Comprehension' is the understanding of what is being read.

At the next level of analysis, we have these activities. Each activity is explained in Table 9.

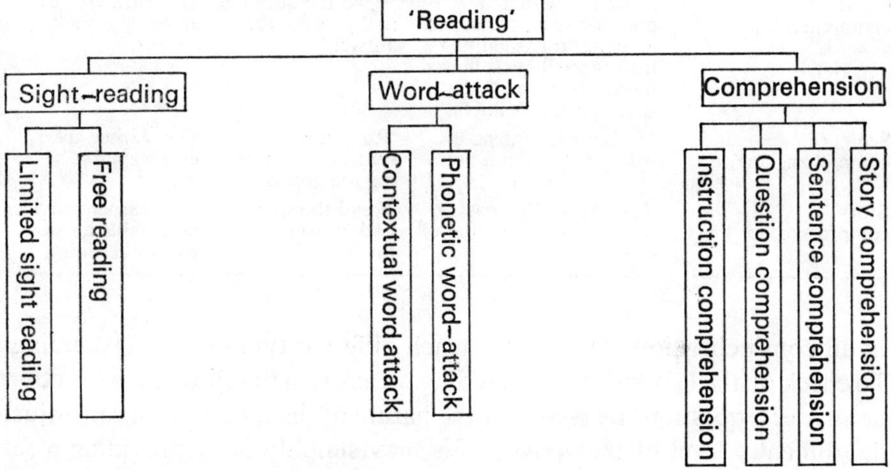

TABLE 9. *Activities in reading*

ACTIVITY	INFORMATION GIVEN TO THE LEARNER	QUESTION ASKED OF THE LEARNER	EXPECTED LEARNER BEHAVIOUR
Limited sight-reading.	Word, phrase, sentence, syllable, or letter with which the learner is already familiar.	The learner is asked to read orally.	Learner reads aloud.
Free reading	Sentences, paragraphs, or stories consisting of familiar words.	The learner is asked to read orally.	Learner reads aloud without long pauses or errors.
Contextual word-attack	A sentence in which a new word is found among familiar ones.	The learner is asked to read the sentence and guess the new word.	The learner reads the entire sentence aloud including the new word.
	An incomplete sentence is given with a strong contextual clue to the missing word. (e.g., 'The plant does not have one leaf. It has two . . . . . .')	The learner is asked to read the sentence and supply a suitable word to complete it.	The learner reads the sentence correctly completing the sentence with a suitable word.
Phonetic word-attack	A new word is given in isolation. This word contains familiar letters in a new combination.	'Read the word aloud.'	The learner reads the word correctly.
Instruction comprehension	A sentence with instruction involving objects (e.g., 'Pick up ruler.') or pictures (e.g., 'Point to zero end of the ruler in the picture.')	'Read the sentence and do what it says.'	The learner performs the activity.

(Continued on the next page.)

ACTIVITY	INFORMATION GIVEN TO THE LEARNER	QUESTION ASKED OF THE LEARNER	EXPECTED LEARNER BEHAVIOUR
Question comprehension	A picture with a question (e.g., picture of a farmer transplanting thakali seedlings followed by the question, 'What is the farmer doing?').	'Read the question and give me the answer.'	The learner gives an acceptable answer.
Sentence comprehension	One or two sentences followed by a question.	'Read the sentences and give me the answer.'	The learner gives an acceptable answer.
Story comprehension	A short reading passage followed by a number of questions.	'Read the story and answer the questions.'	The learner provides acceptable answers to all questions.

In all comprehension activities we teach different types of understanding. To check on the learner's understanding we ask him to follow an instruction or answer a question. By changing the nature of the question we can adjust the difficulty level of the activity. We may simplify it by providing a set of possible answers under the question and have the learner select the best one. We may want the learner to give his own answer. We may require him to provide an oral answer. With an advanced learner, we may require him to write down the correct answer.

We have now chosen the general and specific literacy objectives for our programme based on the level of the learner. The next step is to choose and analyse the linguistic content for these objectives.

How to select the linguistic content

We are now ready to select a set of words and sentence patterns which fit both our learner analysis and subject-matter analysis. The best way to do this is to teach the subject matter to a learner and make a tape recording of the dialogue. This activity is then carried one step farther by requiring the learner to teach the same subject matter to another learner. A recording of this teaching session enables us to identify the natural language used by the learner. This process can be repeated a number of times with new learners teaching still others. If a tape recorder is not available, the programmer can listen and take notes during each teaching session.

How to analyse language elements

Before we can analyse the language samples collected in the previous step, we have to select a basic method for teaching reading. There are many methods of teaching reading and the choice of the best one depends upon the nature of the language. The programming process can be used with any of these different methods.

Having selected a basic method we are now ready to analyse the tape recordings or notes. On the basis of this analysis we identify the following:

Sentences: Basic sentences which present main ideas are identified first. Later, these sentences are divided into phrases, words, syllables and letters.

Words: We make up a list of words required to teach the subject matter. These words are grouped into various categories:
1. Generative words which illustrate regular phonetic principles.
2. Word families with phonetic similarities.
3. Words which fall into grammatic categories (e.g., nouns and verbs).
4. Synonyms and antonyms.
5. Technical terms which are required by the subject matter being taught.

Pictures: Our programme will need pictures to provide clues and to explain the sentences. At this stage of our analysis we make up a list of suitable pictures.

Symbols: In addition to words and pictures, our programme may involve the use of other symbolic elements. Punctuation marks, numerals and map signs are some examples of symbols we may identify at this stage.

Summary

Literacy-skills analysis begins with the selection of a general language objective based on the level of the learner. Specific objectives for sight-reading, word-attack and comprehension are next chosen. Samples of the vocabulary and sentence patterns used in the teaching of the subject matter are collected and analysed into various verbal, pictorial and symbolic elements.

PRACTICAL EXERCISE

Conduct a literacy-skills analysis on the topic you selected for your programme. Use the following steps:

1. *Select a general literacy objective for the programme based upon the literacy skills the learners already have.*
2. *Select specific objectives for reading, word-attack, comprehension and writing.*
3. *Select suitable sentences and words for use in your programme by using the procedure suggested in this chapter.*

CHAPTER FIVE

How are you going to teach?

This chapter discusses the writing of programmes. As we saw in Chapter 1, there are two major types of frames in a programme: teaching frames and test frames. Teaching frames give some information, ask a question based on this information and give the correct answer. Test frames ask a question to check whether the learner has understood the previous teaching frames. Figure 9 shows how these two types of frames are arranged in a programme.

FIGURE 9. *The structure of a programme*

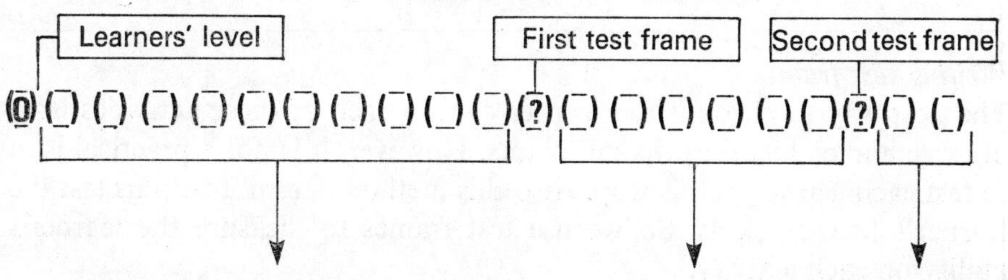

As you can see from the figure, the first set of teaching frames take the learner from what he already knows (his level) to the first test frame. The second set of teaching frames assume that the learner's level has now come up to the first test frame and teaches him new things so that he can answer the second test frame. This process of gradually leading the learner through each test frame is repeated until he can answer all test frames.

General procedure for writing a programme

This list contains various steps in writing a linear programme. Each of these steps is described in detail later:

1. Prepare an instructional sequence.
2. Write test frames for each learning activity.
3. Arrange test frames in an outline of the programme.
4. Revise test frames.
5. Begin at the learner's level and write a set of teaching frames to help him learn how to answer the first test frame. Then write another set of teaching frames to lead the learner to the second test frame. Continue this process to cover all the test frames.

Preparing an instructional sequence
In Chapter 3, we explained how to prepare an instructional sequence from the learning activities. Applying this procedure to the imaginary topic of transplanting thakali seedlings, we produce this instructional sequence:

1. After the first week, thin out seedlings.
2. Recognize when seedlings are ready for transplanting.
3. Dig up seedlings carefully.
4. Replant seedlings at proper depth.
5. Pack the soil tightly around seedlings.

Writing test frames
The best way to check if the learner can do each of these activities is to observe him as he raises thakali plants. However, it is not a practical idea to test each learner in this way. Also this method does not help us test the learner's literacy skills. So we use test frames to measure the learner's ability on each activity.

FIGURE 10. *Test frame at a high level of literacy skill*

What type of thakali plants do you pull out to thin your nursery?

____

____

____

____

____

- -

If many plants are close together, leave the tallest plant. Pull out all other plants. If plants are not close together, do not pull out any plant. Even if the plant is small, leave it alone if it is standing alone.

FIGURE 11. *Test frame at a medium level of literacy skill*

Draw lines to show what you would do with different thakali plants during thinning:

Short plant standing alone.   Pull out a short plant.
Tall plant standing alone.   Pull out a tall plant.
Short plant close to a   Do not pull out the plant.
tall plant.
Two tall plants standing
together.
Two short plants standing
together.

Short plant standing alone.   Pull out a short plant.
Tall plant standing alone?   Pull out a tall plant.
Short plant close to a tall   Do not pull out the plant.
plant.
Two tall plants standing
together.
Two short plants standing
together.

FIGURE 12 .*Test frame at a low level of literacy skill*

In writing these test frames we have to keep in mind the learner's level and our literacy-skills objectives. Taking the first sub-task from the instructional sequence on thakalis, we may use the test frame shown in Figure 10 when we have learners at a high level of literacy skills. With learners at a medium level of literacy skills, our test frame for the same activity will look like Figure 11. Finally, if the learner's level is low, we will use a test frame with very few words as in Figure 12.

Arranging test frames in an outline

If we write a test frame for each learning activity in our instructional sequence, we have a series of test frames which form an outline for our programme. Figure 13 is an example based on the instructional sequence on transplanting thakalis. (The correct answers have not been given in order to save space.)

FIGURE 13. *An outline of test frames*

1

Draw lines to show what you would do with different types of thakali plants during thinning:

Short plant standing alone.	Pull out a short plant.
Tall plant standing alone.	Pull out a tall plant.
Short plant close to a tall plant.	Do not pull out the plant.
Two tall plants standing together.	
Two short plants standing together.	

2

When is a thakali plant ready for transplanting?
Put a (✓) mark in front of the correct answer.

( ) after one week.
( ) after two weeks.
( ) after three weeks.
( ) when the plant has no leaves.
( ) when the plant has two leaves.
( ) when the plant has four leaves.

<hr>

3

Circle TRUE or FALSE:

You should use a rake to dig up thakali plants.   TRUE   FALSE

You should not step on thakali plants.   TRUE   FALSE

You should cut the root of the plant when
you dig it up.   TRUE   FALSE

You should dig up one plant at a time.   TRUE   FALSE

<hr>

4

How deep do we transplant thakali?

Put a   (✓)   mark in front of the correct answer.

( )   cover the roots.

( )   cover the stem up to the first set of leaves.

( )   cover the stem up to the second set of leaves.

<hr>

5

What should you do as soon as you transplant?

Put a   ✓   mark in front of the correct answer.

( )   pour water.

( )   stamp on the plant.

( )   stamp on the soil around the plant.

<hr>

Although we write all test frames at the same time, they will not be placed together in the final programme. (The numbers for the test frame are only to help you compare them with the instructional sequence given earlier.) In the actual programme, there will be a number of teaching frames between one test frame and the next one.

Revising test frames

Before writing our teaching frames, it is a good idea to take a look at our test-frame outline and make any necessary revisions. Table 10 is a checklist for evaluating test frames.

TABLE 10. *A checklist for evaluating test frames*

QUESTION	REVISION
1. Is there a test frame for each activity in the instructional sequence?	If not, write more test frames as needed.
2. Do the test frames take the literacy-skills objectives into account?	If not, revise the test frames so that they require literacy skills at the suitable level.
3. Do the test frames progress from simple to complex tasks?	If not, rearrange the test frames into a more gradual sequence.
4. Does the test frame contain any new information?	If so, remove the information from the frame. Remember, new information is presented in teaching frames. The test frame merely checks to see if the student has learned all important points from previous teaching frames.

Writing teaching frames

We write a set of teaching frames to help the learner to move from what he already knows to the first test frame. We then write another set of teaching frames to take him to the next test frame, and so on, until all test frames are covered. The number of teaching frames between any two test frames depends upon the difficulty of the learning activity. Usually from five to fifteen teaching frames will be enough to lead the learner from one test frame to another.

Here is an example of the procedure for writing teaching frames. We assume that the learner already knows how to recognize a thakali plant. However, he does not know the importance of transplanting thakali seedlings. Nor does he know the procedure for transplanting. His reading level is fairly high but his writing skills are not. Our first task in writing the teaching frames is to take the learner to this first test frame (Figure 14).

FIGURE 14. *A first test frame on thakali plants*

You are thinning thakali plants. Draw lines to show what you would do with different types of thakali plants.

A short plant standing alone.	Pull out a short plant.
A tall plant standing alone.	Pull out a tall plant.
A short plant close to a tall plant.	
	Do not pull out the plant.
Two tall plants standing together.	
Two short plants standing together.	

Figure 15 is a sample set of teaching frames to close the gap between what the learner already knows and the first test frame. (To save space the correct answers have not been given.) The first frame begins with what the learner already knows. It motivates him with a picture of a healthy plant with many fruits. It asks a simple question for which the correct answer is obvious. The learner does not have to read and understand any complex sentences. In the second frame the idea of thinning the plants is introduced, for which reasons are given in Frame 3. The sequence continues as follows: Frame 4 introduces the fact that the farmer does the thinning; Frame 5 introduces a rule for thinning—do not pull out any single plants—and uses underlined words to give a clue; Frame 6 reinforces the information presented in the previous frame using a picture instead of words; Frame 7 introduces the second rule of thinning—in a crowd of plants, leave the tallest one; Frame 8 reviews what was taught in the previous one and prepares the learner for the test frame; Frame 9 is our first test frame. Notice that the frame gets the next number in the sequence (9) and there is nothing to tell the learner that it is different from previous frames. If the eight teaching frames have performed their function, the learner should have no difficulty in giving the correct answer to the test frame.

We are now ready to write another set of teaching frames to take the learner to the second test frame. After that we repeat this process until the learner can answer all test frames in the programme.

FIGURE 15. *A sample set of teaching frames*

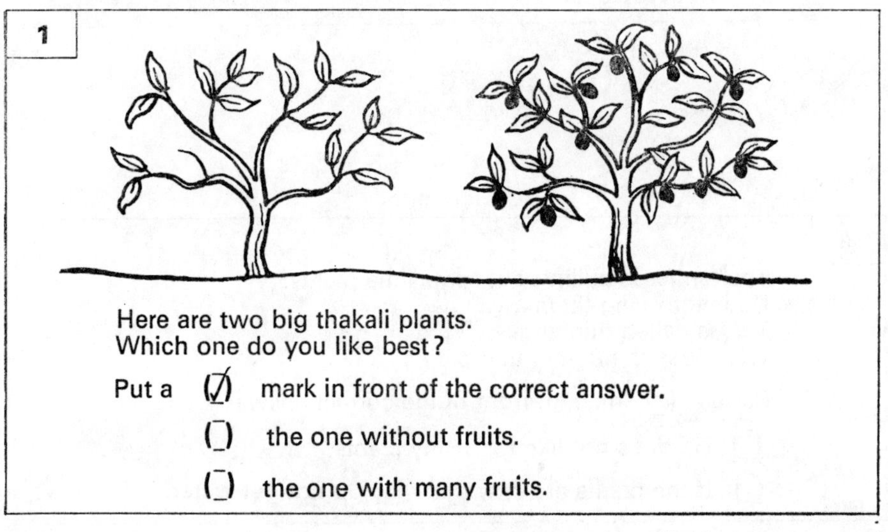

(Continued on the next page.)

2

A big thakali plant begins with a small one.
We pull out some of the small plants and throw them away.
We have 20 small plants.
How many big plants will we have?

Put a (✓) mark in front of the correct answer.

( ) More than 20
( ) 20
( ) Less than 20

3

The farmer sows thakali seeds.
This is the end of the first week.
Little plants need water.
The plants will get more water if they are ________

Put a (✓) mark in front of the correct answer.

( ) crowded.
( ) not crowded.

4

The farmer is pulling out some little plants.
He is throwing them away.
This is called thinning.
Why does the farmer thin plants?

Put a (✓) mark in front of the correct answer.

( ) He does not like too many plants.

( ) If the plants are crowded they do not get water.

(Continued on the next page.)

5

Thinning makes plants less crowded.

If there is a <u>single</u> plant standing alone, does the farmer pull it out?

Put a ☑ mark in front of the correct answer.

( ) No, because it is not crowded.

( ) Yes.

6

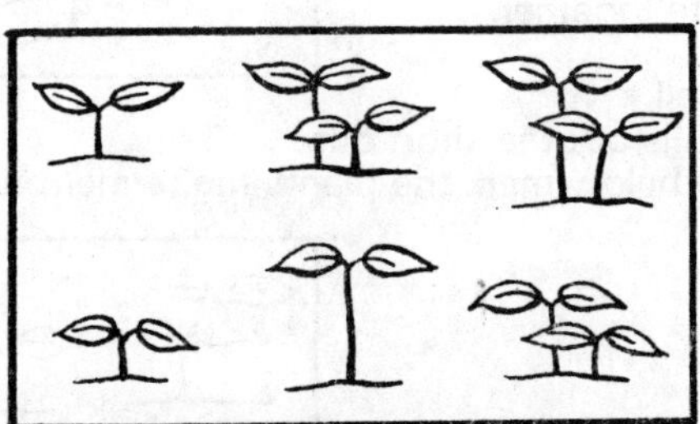

Here are some thakali plants at the end of the first week.

The farmer does not pull out plants standing alone.

Put a circle around the plants the farmer does <u>not</u> pull out.

7

Two plants are close together.
The taller plant is stronger.
Stronger plants give more fruit.
The farmer pulls out one of the plants.
Which one does he pull out?

Put a ☑ mark in front of the correct answer.

( ) He pulls out the tall plant.

( ) He pulls out the short plant.

(Continued on the next page.)

8

Two plants are together.
They are the same size.
The farmer may pull out any one of them.

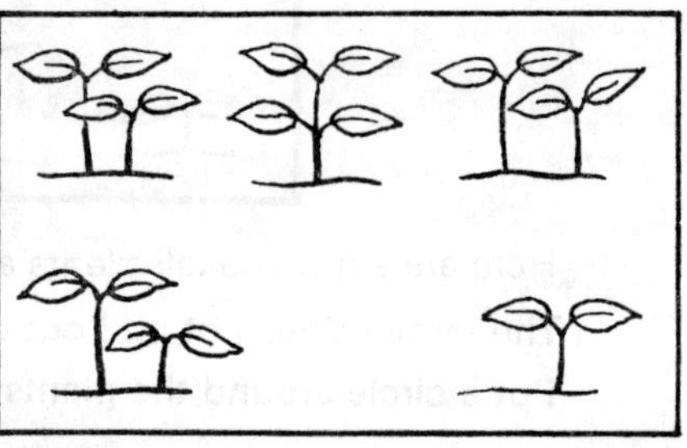

Two plants are together.
One is short.
The other is tall.
The farmer pulls out the short one.
In the picture below mark the plants the farmer pulls out.

9

You are thinning thakali plants.
Draw lines to show what you would do with different types of thakali plants.

A short plant standing alone.   Pull out a short plant.
A tall plant standing alone.   Pull out a tall plant.
A short plant close to a tall   Do not pull out the
plant.   plant.
Two tall plants standing together.
Two short plants standing together.

Revising teaching frames

Each teaching frame contains three parts: information, question and correct answer. In the sample set of teaching frames shown in Figure 15 we used only a limited variety of these three parts. In the following sections we discuss different methods of presenting information, asking a question and providing the correct answer.

Presenting information

Here are a number of different ways in which new information can be presented in teaching frames:

1. *Actual objects:* The teaching frame may ask the learner to study an actual object. This method should apply when the learner has a limited vocabulary or when the programme deals with the use of the object. For example, in teaching learners how to use a spray pump, we may ask the learner to get hold of an actual pump and study the different parts.

2. *Photographs and pictures:* Photographs are useful in presenting such information as the appearance of an insect. However, they are usually expensive. Pictures are easier to draw and to reproduce. These pictures should be simple and direct rather than artistic. Many programmers mistakenly assume that everybody can understand a picture. Actually, visual literacy or the ability to 'read' a picture is a skill which has to be taught.

3. *Examples:* In many instances, examples and stories can be used to present new information to the learners. These stories are more interesting and meaningful than abstract principles.

Asking questions

From the point of view of literacy skills, we may divide the questions used in a programme into two major categories: (a) selection questions which require reading comprehension skills; and (b) direct questions which require writing skills. All questions used in the sample frames are selection questions. In these questions, the learner merely has to read and recognize the correct answer. In contrast to this, direct questions require the learner to write the answer. Within each of these two major categories there are a number of different forms:

1. *Selection questions:*
    (a) Figure 16 is an example of a multiple-choice question. Usually, there is only one correct answer among the alternatives. If more than one correct answer is to be found (as in this example) the learner

should be told about it. In writing multiple-choice questions, the programmer should select his incorrect answers carefully so that they require the right amount of reading comprehension. In Figure 16, a high level of reading comprehension is required. With readers at a lower level we can make the incorrect answers easier to recognize. We may also give fewer answers to choose from.

(b) Figure 17 is an example of a true-false question. Instead of the TRUE and FALSE, we may use YES and NO. It is a good idea to have equal numbers of true and false statements.

(c) Figure 18 is an example of a matching question. This is a familiar example. The learner reads each statement in the first column and chooses a matching statement from the next one. It is not necessary for both columns to have the same number of statements. As our example shows, the same item in one column can be matched with different items in the other.

(d) Figure 19 is an example of a sequencing question. This format is useful whenever the sequence of activities is important.

2. *Direct questions:*
 (a) An example of a regular question is given in Figure 20.
 (b) Figure 21 illustrates a completion question.

FIGURE 16. *A multiple-choice question*

In thinning thakali plants what does the farmer do?

Put a (✓) mark in front of two correct answers:
( ) Pull out all short plants.
( ) Pull out all tall plants.
( ) Pull out short and tall plants which stand alone.
( ) Pull out short plants which stand close to a tall one.
( ) Pull out tall plants which stand close to another tall one.

- -

( ) Pull out all short plants.
( ) Pull out all tall plants.
( ) Pull out short and tall plants which stand alone.
(✓) Pull out short plants which stand close to a tall one.
(✓) Pull out tall plants which stand close to another tall one.

FIGURE 17. *A true-false question*

Read each of the following sentences. Underline the word TRUE if the sentence is true. If not, underline the word FALSE.

1. Short plants are pulled out if they stand alone. — TRUE   FALSE
2. Short plants are pulled out if they stand close to a tall one. — TRUE   FALSE
3. Tall plants are always pulled out. — TRUE   FALSE
4. Tall plants are pulled out if they stand close to a short one. — TRUE   FALSE

- -

1. Short plants are pulled out if they stand alone. — TRUE   <u>FALSE</u>
2. Short plants are pulled out if they stand close to a tall one. — <u>TRUE</u>   FALSE
3. Tall plants are always pulled out. — TRUE   <u>FALSE</u>
4. Tall plants are pulled out if they stand close to a short one. — TRUE   <u>FALSE</u>

FIGURE 18. *A matching question*

Draw lines to connect what the farmer would do with different types of thakali plants:

A short plant standing alone. — Pull out a short plant.
A tall plant standing alone. — Pull out a tall plant.
A short plant standing next to a tall plant. — Do not pull out the plant.
Two tall plants standing together.

- -

A short plant standing alone. — Pull out a short plant.
A tall plant standing alone. — Pull out a tall plant.
A short plant standing next to a tall plant. — Do not pull out the plant.
Two tall plants standing together.

FIGURE 19. *A sequencing question*

These are five different things a farmer does in growing thakali plants. They are not in the correct order. Write the numbers 1, 2, 3, 4, and 5 in front of each sentence to show the correct order:

_______________ The farmer thins the plants.
_______________ The farmer digs out the plant after three weeks.
_______________ The farmer sows the seed.
_______________ The farmer stamps on the soil around the plant.
_______________ The farmer places the plant in a deeper hole.

_______2_______ The farmer thins the plant.
_______3_______ The farmer digs out the plant after three weeks.
_______1_______ The farmer sows the seed.
_______5_______ The farmer stamps on the soil around the plant.
_______4_______ The farmer places the plant in a deeper hole.

FIGURE 20. *A regular question*

What are the important things to remember in thinning thakali plants?

____

____

____

____

____

1. Plants which stand alone should not be pulled out.
2. In a group of plants, leave the tallest plant. Pull out all other plants.
(Your answer may use different words, but say the same thing.)

FIGURE 21. *A completion question*

Pulling out some plants to reduce crowding is called_________.

Pulling out some plants to reduce crowding is called thinning.

Providing the correct answer

Providing the correct answer is an important principle of programmed instruction. The learner feels a sense of pride if he finds his answer the same as the correct-answer feedback. If they differ, the learner can re-read the frame and correct his mistake before it becomes more confusing. With selection questions, it is a good idea to reproduce the entire question with the correct answer clearly indicated. With direct questions, we may just show the correct answer. If a lengthy answer is required the learner should be told that his answer need not use the same words. The correct answer is best printed on the back of the frame so that the learner does not accidentally see it before he has given his answer.

Prompting

When you are revising your frames it is important to check if the difficulty level of the question is suited to the level of the learner. With beginning learners we may give various hints or 'prompts' to simplify the question. Pictures provide useful prompts. They may be used to introduce a new word:

There are many other kinds of prompts. By printing the word 'blue' in blue ink and 'red' in red ink, we can prompt the reading of names of different colours. Arrows, underlining and other printed clues are also used as prompts. Another type of prompt provides parts of a word the learner is required to recall:

> We are now ready to trans_____the thakali plant.

Sometimes you may use the structure of the sentence to provide a prompt:

> The root is under the ground.
>
> Most of the stem is also ______ / ______ / ______

As you can see, prompts help the learner associate what he already knows (e.g., identify blue colour) to some new knowledge or skill (e.g., read the printed word 'blue'). Prompts also help the learner recall information from previous frames.

There is a danger in using too many prompts. We do not want the learner to use them as crutches and never learn how to answer without them. We cannot keep on printing a picture every time we use the word 'spade'. So it is important to remove the prompts as soon as possible and require the learner to give his own answers. The process of gradually removing the prompts is called 'fading'.

Let us assume that we are teaching the learner how to read the word 'blue'. We begin by printing the entire word in blue ink. In the next frame, we merely print the initial letter 'b' in blue ink and the rest of the word in black ink. Finally, we present the student with the word 'blue' in black without any prompts.

Figure 22 is another example of the 'fading' of prompts. This time we are trying to teach the learner how to spell the word 'transplant'.

FIGURE 22. *'Fading' prompts*

1. We <u>transplant</u> small plants. Write this   word: ________
2. We transplant a small <u>plant</u>. After we trans_____, the plant grows bigger.
3. If we do not_____plant a plant, it does not grow big.
4. John has small plants. He is ready to ____________

Assembling the programme

After revising the frames so that they contain the most effective method for presenting information, asking questions, prompting and giving the correct answer, we are ready to assemble them into a programmed book. At this stage of production, it is a good idea to keep each frame on a separate sheet of paper with the information and the question on one side and the correct answer on the back. This arrangement makes it easy to add or remove frames during the try-outs.

Summary

In this chapter we presented the procedure for designing a programme. The major steps in this procedure include:

1. Arranging the learning activities into a suitable instructional sequence.
2. Writing a test frame to measure the attainment of each activity.
3. Arranging the test frames into an outline of the programme.
4. Revising the test frames.
5. Writing teaching frames to take the learner gradually from his beginning level to all test frames.
6. Revising each teaching frame so that it uses the most appropriate method for presenting information and the most suitable form of question.
7. Assembling the frames into a programmed book.

Although you may believe that your programme is complete now, there is still a long way to go. The programme has to be evaluated and revised to make it more effective.

PRACTICAL EXERCISE

This is a lengthy assignment in which you prepare the first version of your programme. Here are the various steps of this exercise:

1. *Study the instructional sequence which you prepared in the subject-matter analysis exercise at the end of Chapter 3. Check the test items for each learning activity and make suitable changes if necessary.*
2. *Arrange the test frames into an outline for the programme.*
3. *Check your learner analysis from the exercise at the end of Chapter 2 to find out what the learner already knows about the subject matter. Write a series of teaching frames to take the learner on from this level to each of the test frames.*
4. *Revise each teaching frame so that it uses the most suitable language and types of questions.*
5. *Assemble the frames into a programmed book.*

CHAPTER SIX

How to revise your programme

When you complete the writing of the programme you may feel that you have finished your task. However, you still have a long way to go in the programming process. You have to improve the first version of your programme by repeatedly revising it. There are two basic methods for making these revisions, each of which we will discuss in more detail:

1. *Expert evaluation.* You show the programme to such experts as functional literacy workers, linguists and the local agricultural officers. You make changes on the basis of their suggestions.
2. *Learner try-out.* You actually use the programme with some learners. You make changes on the basis of the problems which arise during these try-out sessions.

Expert evaluation

You will need three kinds of experts for this purpose: (a) subject-matter experts; (b) community experts; and (c) literacy experts. Here are some methods for obtaining useful suggestions from these experts:

1. Use more than one expert to obtain more suggestions. You do not have to follow all of their suggestions; you can choose those which are practical.
2. Ask each expert to evaluate within his own field. For example, it is not necessary to have the agricultural expert make suggestions about grammar. An effective way to focus each expert's attention is to use a questionnaire.
3. Your experts may not know anything about programmed instructi on You may have to explain how the materials are to be used by the learners.
4. It is a good idea to begin with an evaluation of the subject-matter programme by technical experts. These experts should be given copies of the programme and a questionnaire similar to the one in Figure 23.

5. Functional literacy experts evaluate the practical use of the pro-
    gramme. In this process, they take into account the subject matter,
    the language and the format of the programme. The sample question-
    naire in Figure 24 shows how this type of evaluation is undertaken.
6. You may have to change the language of the programme when you
    revise it on the basis of the above evaluations. This is why evaluation
    by language experts is undertaken last. The purpose of this evaluation
    is to check if the level, style and vocabulary of the programme are
    suited to the community. Figure 25 is a sample questionnaire for the
    language experts.

Learner try-outs

Your experts may make suggestions for improving the programme and
you may carry out all of them. However, there is no guarantee that the
programme is an effective one unless it is tried out with actual learners.
During these try-outs you make use of what the learner says and does in
order to revise your programme. In general, you do three different things:
(a) carefully watch what the learner actually does (e.g., he makes a mistake
on Frame 4 and complains that the programme is too easy); (b) identify
problem areas of the programme (e.g., Frame 4 is too difficult but the
programme as a whole is too easy); and (c) revise the programme (e.g.,
add a prompt to Frame 4 and reduce the total number of teaching frames).
You should remember that you are testing the programme and not the
learner. If the learner makes a mistake it is not his fault, but a fault of
the programme.

There are three phases in trying out a programme. Each has a different
procedure and collects different types of information. In the first phase,
you try out the programme on a single learner from your community. On
the basis of his responses, remarks and reactions, you make revisions
and try it out on another learner. This procedure of revising and re-
testing the programme is repeated until you get satisfactory results.

In the second phase of trying out, you test the revised programme with
a group of learners. You study the errors made by all learners and then
make suitable revisions.

In the third phase, you remove yourself from the testing procedure and
let someone else test the programme under actual field conditions. Using
reports and suggestions from this evaluator you revise the programme to
make it more usable by others. Here are more specific suggestions for each
phase of trying out.

FIGURE 23. *Sample questionnaire for the evaluation of the subject matter of the programme*

EVALUATION QUESTIONNAIRE I

Subject matter

The following programme deals with the care of new-born babies. It is designed for use by rural mothers. Although there will be a teacher, the learner will work through the programme alone. Please study the programme carefully and answer each of the following questions by making a √ mark next to YES or NO.

1. Do you feel that the subject matter of the programme will help the community?
   ___________ YES ___________ NO

2. Will adult women feel that the subject matter is important to them?
   ___________ YES ___________ NO

3. Does the programme give correct information?
   ___________ YES ___________ NO

4. Is the programme easy to understand?
   ___________ YES ___________ NO

5. Are the technical words clearly explained?
   ___________ YES ___________ NO

6. Does the programme contain enough examples?
   ___________ YES ___________ NO

7. Are the examples meaningful to women learners?
   ___________ YES ___________ NO

Please write down any suggestions for improving the programme.
1. What incorrect and unnecessary information should be removed from the programme?

   ....

   ....

2. What additional information should be included?

   ....

(Continued on the next page.)

3. What additional examples should be given?

    ....

4. How can the programme be made more interesting to the
    women learners?

    ....

    ....

FIGURE 24. *Sample questionnaire for evaluating the usability of a programme*

EVALUATION QUESTIONNAIRE II

Usability of the programme

The following programme is on taking care of new-born babies.
It is designed for use by rural mothers. The programme is to be used
mostly by the learners themselves with very little help from a
teacher. Please study the programme carefully and answer the
following questions:

1. Is the objective of the programme meaningful to the woman
learner?

    ______________ YES ______________ NO

2. Are the literacy skills taught in the programme suitable for
    the learner?

    ______________ YES ______________ NO

3. Is the length of the programme suitable?

    ______________ YES ______________ NO

4. Is the language used in the programme clear?

    ______________ YES ______________ NO

5. Can the learner use the programme without a teacher?

    ______________ YES ______________ NO

6. Will the teacher be able to explain how to use the programme?

    ______________ YES ______________ NO

(Continued on the next page.)

7. Does the teacher require any special training to use the programme?
    _______________ YES _______________ NO

8. Is the programme inexpensive?
    _______________ YES _______________ NO

9. Would you use the programme with your learners?
    _______________ YES _______________ NO

After answering these questions, please list any suggestions for making the programme more usable:

....

....

....

FIGURE 25. *Sample questionnaire for evaluating the language used in the programme*

EVALUATION QUESTIONNAIRE III

Language

The following programme deals with the care of new-born babies. It is also designed to help rural women improve their vocabulary and reading comprehension in the area of child care. The users of the programme have very few basic literacy skills. They are expected to use the programme without much help from a teacher. Please study the programme carefully and answer the following questions by placing a √ mark in front of the appropriate choice:

1. Length of the programme:
    ( ) Too long   ( ) Too short   ( ) Right length

2. Writing style:
    ( ) Clear   ( ) Confusing

3. Introduction of new words:
    ( ) Effective   ( ) Ineffective

4. Repetition of new words:
    ( ) Too little   ( ) Too much   ( ) Right amount

(Continued on the next page.)

5. Use of technical vocabulary:
    (   )   Easy to understand   (   )   Hard to understand

6. Style of language:
    (   )   Too formal   (   )   Too colloquial   (   )   Appropriate

7. Use of illustrations:
    (   )   Suitable   (   )   Distracting

8. Number of questions:
    (   )   Too few   (   )   Too many   (   )   Right number

9. Type of questions:
    (   )   Too easy   (   )   Too difficult (   )   Right level

10. Type of sentences:
    (   )   Appropriate   (   )   Inappropriate

11. Sequence and organization:
    (   )   Smooth   (   )   Disconnected

Phase I: Individual testing

Who should do the testing?

The programmer is the best person to test the programme with individual learners. He can watch the learner's reactions and listen to his remarks during the try-out. For example, a learner may indicate his boredom by yawning repeatedly or by staring out of the window. It is impossible to record and report all this information to the programmer when someone else does the testing. Also when the programmer conducts his own testing, he sees the effects of everything he has done so far. Sometimes this is a rewarding experience and at other times there are major problems. As the programme improves through revisions, so does the programmer. Very often a learner may get stuck on a frame and the programmer can make minor revisions in the frame. This gives him an opportunity to test the revised frame immediately.

What type of learners is involved?

The main purpose of this phase of try-out is to discover major problems in the programme. You need learners who are capable of expressing such problems. About four or five such learners from the community are usually sufficient for this type of try-out.

Preparing the programme

The programme should be typewritten or neatly handwritten in a readable form before being given to the learner. Each frame of the programme should be on a separate sheet of paper so that, when you revise or remove a frame, you do not have to reproduce the entire programme. You will also need two copies of the programme—one for the learner and one for you. As the learner goes through his frames you can make notes on the other. If the learner is unable to answer a frame, you can make suitable changes on your copy. You do not have to include the correct answer to each frame because you can give this information directly to the learner.

If someone else is conducting the first phase of testing on your programme, the form on Figure 26 will be useful for reporting this information. Each teaching and test frame is clearly identified in this form. There are two columns for each frame, one for the learner's answer and the other for his reaction. In the first column the symbols $\sqrt{}$ and X indicate correct and incorrect answers, respectively. Additional information about these answers may be recorded with the following symbols:

$\sqrt{}$ = correct answers given immediately;

$*$ = incorrect answer given immediately;

$\sqrt{}\sqrt{}$ = correct answer given after a pause;

X X = incorrect answer given after a pause;

X $\sqrt{}$ = incorrect answer given first. Learner corrects himself later.

In the second column, the symbols + or — indicate a positive or negative comment made by the student.

Conducting the try-out

The purpose of these try-outs is to collect information for the improvement of the programme. You should make sure that the learner understands this. Do not show any displeasure if the learner makes a mistake. Explain to him that he has provided useful information for the improvement of the programme and resist the temptation to teach the learner whenever he hesitates or makes a mistake. Instead of telling him the correct answer, revise the frame and try it out again. If the learner hesitates over a question for a long time, ask him to 'think aloud' and explain his problems. When he does this, you may be able to make changes on the duplicate frame. You can also add a frame, or divide a frame into two parts. These on-the-spot revisions are important in this first phase of try-outs.

Another important fact for you to remember during these try-outs is that your job is to watch and not to teach. You will have to explain to the

FIGURE 26. *Sample form for programme tester (Numbers in circle indicate test frames)*

Students	Frames									
	1	2	3	4	(5)	6	7	8	(9)	10
1. A.B.										
2. S.T.										
3. T.J.										
4. C.C.										
5. A.L.										
6. P.M.										
7. L.T.										
8. R.R.										
9. S.K.										
10. P.K.										

learner how to use the programme, but after that do not talk unless absolutely necessary. Pull out your set of duplicate frames and take notes about the reactions and comments of the learner. However, the learner may not offer any suggestions out of his respect for you, so to encourage him, you may leave some obvious mistake in the first few frames so that the learner can point this out.

You should pay special attention to the test frames. If the learner makes an error in a *teaching* frame, you modify that frame. However, if he makes an error in a *test* frame, do not simplify the question. Instead, revise the teaching frames which come before that test frame.

Concluding the try-out

It is not a good idea to continue a try-out for more than forty-five minutes, because a tired learner does not give you useful information. When you stop testing in the middle of a programme, be sure to do so at a test frame. The learner can begin with a new set of teaching frames in the next session.

After you have completed the testing of the entire programme, take some time to talk to the learner about his experience. Ask him how he felt while studying the programme and which sections were difficult or confusing. You may also take the learner through the test frames once again to see if he can still answer them correctly.

Making revisions

During the first phase of try-outs you have made minor and major changes in the copy of your programme as the learner works through his. Immediately after the try-out session you should complete all revisions, clean up the frames and prepare the programme for the next round of testing.

Phase II: Group testing

The first phase of try-outs helps you to identify the major problems in your programme. After four or five of these individual try-out sessions, you should have made most major revisions. You are now ready to move into the second phase in which information is collected from a group of learners to identify further changes needed in the programme. Suggestions for this phase of try-outs are given on following pages.

Who are involved in testing?
This phase of testing does not require careful observations of each student. Between ten to fifty learners make up a useful test group.

Preparing the programme
Multiple copies of the programme should be cyclostyled in its final format. At this stage, each frame need not be on a separate sheet of paper. Correct answers should be included in each frame.

Conducting the try-out
Before the try-out, you should write a 'teacher's manual' with specific instructions on how to introduce the programme to the learners, explain its use and provide help to learners. During the actual use of the programme you should follow these instructions because you are trying them out also. Ask your learners to answer the questions on each frame. If they want to change an answer, they should do so without erasing the original answer. You should also keep track of how much time each learner needed to work through the programme.

Concluding the try-out
Some of your learners will finish the programme ahead of others. You may talk to them about their experiences. Do not hurry up the slower learners or start teaching them yourself.

Making revisions
After the try-out you should collect all copies of the programme. Learners' answers from these programmes provide useful information for new revisions. You can analyse the answers by using the summary table shown in Figure 27. The columns in this table represent different frames and the rows stand for different learners participating in the tryout. The √ or X symbols indicate whether or not the learner gave the correct answer to the question. Table 11 indicates the suitable types of revisions for various patterns of errors.

FIGURE 27. *Sample summary table showing correct (✓) and incorrect (x) answers given by learners*

Students							Frames													
	1	2	3	4	5	6	7	8	9	10	11	12	13	14	15	16	17	18	19	20
1. G.G.	✓	✓	✓	✓	✓	✓	✓	✓	✓	✗	✓	✓	✓	✓	✓	✓	✓	✓	✓	✓
2. N.V.	✓	✓	✗	✓	✗	✓	✓	✗	✓	✓	✓	✓	✓	✓	✗	✓	✓	✓	✓	✓
3. C.W.	✓	✗	✗	✓	✓	✓	✓	✓	✓	✓	✓	✓	✓	✗	✓	✓	✓	✗	✓	✗
4. S.C.	✓	✓	✗	✓	✓	✓	✓	✗	✓	✓	✗	✓	✓	✓	✗	✓	✓	✓	✓	✓
5. T.R.	✓	✓	✓	✓	✓	✓	✓	✗	✓	✓	✓	✗	✓	✓	✗	✓	✓	✗	✓	✓
6. T.D.	✓	✓	✗	✓	✓	✓	✓	✓	✓	✓	✓	✓	✓	✓	✓	✓	✓	✓	✓	✓
7. G.N.	✓	✓	✗	✓	✓	✓	✓	✗	✓	✓	✓	✓	✓	✓	✗	✓	✓	✗	✓	✓
8. I.T.	✓	✓	✓	✓	✓	✓	✓	✗	✓	✓	✓	✓	✓	✓	✗	✓	✓	✗	✓	✓
9. R.M.	✓	✓	✗	✓	✓	✓	✓	✓	✓	✓	✓	✓	✓	✓	✓	✓	✓	✓	✓	✓
10. K.B.	✓	✓	✗	✓	✓	✓	✓	✓	✓	✓	✓	✓	✓	✓	✗	✓	✓	✗	✓	✓

TABLE 11. *Suggested revisions for different types of error patterns*

PATTERN OF ERROR	EXAMPLE FROM THE SUMMARY TABLE (FIGURE 27)	SUGGESTED REVISION
Teaching frames with a small number of errors.	1, 2, 4	No revision necessary.
Teaching frames with a large number of errors.	3	Divide the frame into more than one frame. Add prompts or illustrations to the frame. Simplify the language used in the frame. Check to see if the errors indicate the same type of misunderstanding. If so, design a branching segment (see Chapter 7).
Errors made by about half of the learners.	8, 18	Add a wash-ahead sequence to provide more practice for those who need it (see Chapter 7). Check to see if the learners lack specific entry skills. If so, design a supplementary programme to be taken before starting this programme.
Test frames with a small number of errors.	7	No revision needed.
Test frames with a large number of errors.	15	Make the question clearer. If the question is clear enough, check the teaching frames which lead up to that test frame. Increase the number of teaching frames. Provide more practice to the learners. See if there is any specific teaching frame which is missed by the learners (e.g., Frame 8 in the chart). This could be the critical frame which needs revision.

Phase III: Field testing

In this phase of trying out your programme you check to see how it
works in other people's hands.

Who are the people involved?

For this phase of testing you will need a teacher who is willing to help
you by keeping detailed records about the effects of the programme. This
teacher should have adult learners from the same community.

Preparing the programme

The programme is revised on the basis of the information collected during the previous phases and reproduced in a neat format. In addition, you should also prepare a set of instructions which tells the teacher how to use the programme.

How to conduct the try-out

The procedure followed in this phase is the same as in the previous one, except you are not directly involved in the try-out. This teacher follows instructions as closely as possible. He may make some changes in the programme or in the way it is used, provided he makes a note of it. The teacher also keeps a log or a diary of his experiences, including problems reported by the students.

Concluding the try-out

As soon as all learners complete the programme, the teacher collects the copies. When all students have finished, the teacher prepares another summary chart as was shown in Figure 27. You receive this chart along with the teacher's diary of experiences. You may supplement these with a chat with the teacher. Based on all these pieces of information, you make the final revisions on the programme.

This is the end of the try-out stage in the programming process. However, the revision of the programme never comes to an end. When you use the programme with new learners or send it out for use by other literacy workers, you continue to collect information on its effectiveness.

Summary

Expert evaluation and try-outs of a programme are conducted for the purpose of improving its effectiveness. Table 12 summarizes the purposes of different types of expert evaluation.

TABLE 12. *Summary of expert evaluation*

TYPE OF EXPERT	PURPOSE OF EVALUATION
1. Subject-matter expert	To identify any error in the subject matter of the programme. To improve the explanations and examples used in the programme.
2. Community expert	To check the usability of the programme in the community.
3. Language specialists	To check the suitability of the level and style of the language of the programme. To improve the effectiveness of the programme in teaching literacy skills.

Trying out the programme involves learners. However, its function is not to test the learners but to measure the effects of the programme. Table 13 summarizes the three phases of tryouts.

TABLE 13. *Summary of try-out phases*

PHASE	STUDENTS	SITUATION	MODIFICATIONS
1. Individual testing.	Four or five learners tested singly.	Face-to-face testing by programmer.	Changes made on the spot while the learner works through the programme.
2. Group testing.	A small group of learners.	Actual classroom situation.	Changes made on the basis of an analysis of learner's answers.
3. Field testing.	Learners in existing programmes.	Actual use by literacy worker without any help from the programmer.	Changes based on the reports of the literacy worker and learners' answers.

Trying out the programme is the most important element of the programming process. By involving the learner early in the development of the programme and by carefully studying his reactions, remarks and responses, we make him our collaborator!

PRACTICAL EXERCISE

For this exercise you will need the help of other experts and literacy workers. Here are the specific steps:

1. *Show your first version of the programme to one or more subject-matter experts (e.g., agricultural officers), community experts (e.g., village headmen) and language specialists (e.g., linguists). Make suitable changes in the programme on the basis of their suggestions.*

2. *Show the revised version of your programme to four or five learners from the community, one at a time. Make suitable changes on the basis of their comments and answers.*

3. *Test the programme with a group of learners. Make suitable changes by studying their answers.*

4. *Send the programme to another literacy worker if possible. Make changes based on his report.*

CHAPTER SEVEN

Other types of programmed instruction

There are many different kinds of programmes. The type of programme described so far is called 'linear'. If the squares in the following figure represent frames and the arrows indicate the path taken by the learner, the structure of a linear programme may be shown this way:

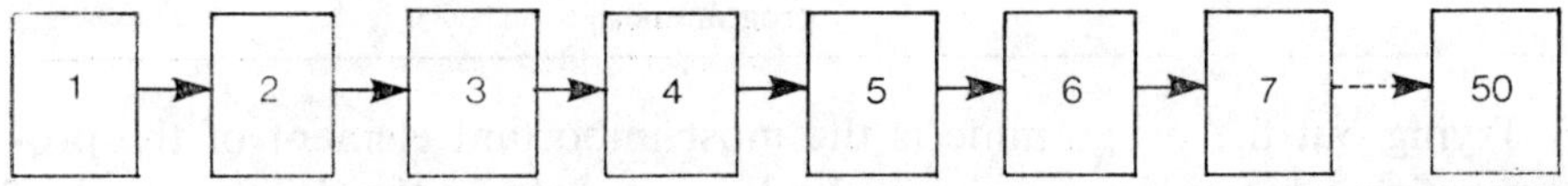

A linear programme permits the learner to work at his own speed. However, it does not take into account other differences among learners.

Variations of linear programmes

Wash-back and wash-ahead programmes
A variation of the linear programme is called a wash-back programme as shown in the following diagram:

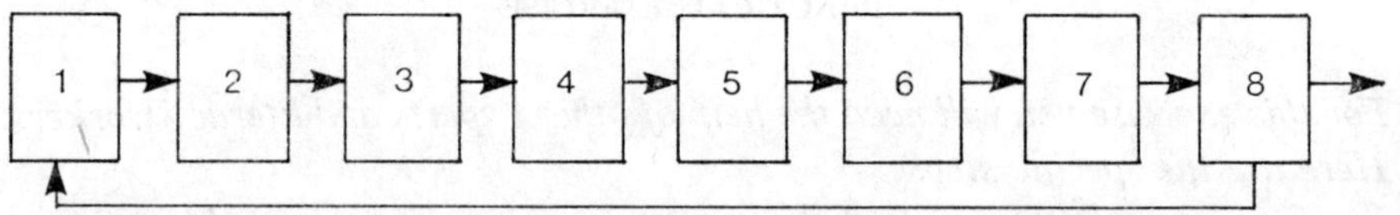

Instructions on Frame 8 in this sequence ask the learner to return to the first frame if he made an error. If the learner gave the correct answer, he moves to the next frame. In this way, the wash-back programme takes into account different amounts of practice needed by different learners.

To adjust for differences in what the learners already know, a slightly different arrangement called a wash-ahead programme is used:

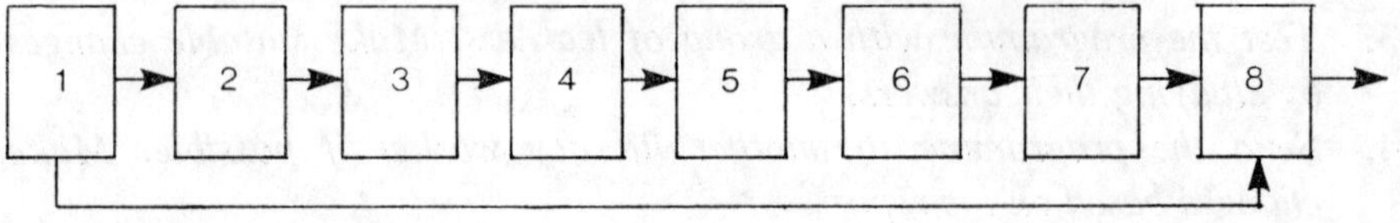

The first frame is a test frame which checks to see if the learner knows some basic concept. For example, this first frame checks to see if the student knows how to use a ruler correctly (Figure 28). If the learner does not choose the correct answer, he is taught the necessary concept in the next six frames. If he chooses the correct answer, he goes directly to Frame 8 which begins the next unit.

FIGURE 28. *A first frame to check learner's knowledge level*

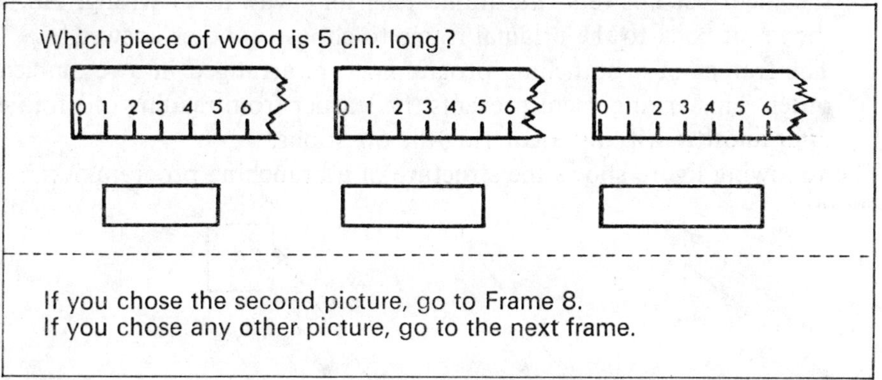

Multiple-track programmes
To adjust for different language and learning levels, another variation of the linear programme, called a multiple-track programme, is used. Its structure is shown in the following figure:

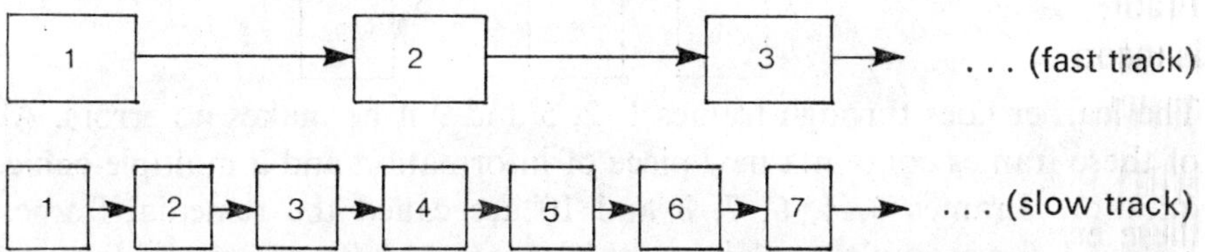

In this type of programme, the top frame on each page is at a high language level. If the learner is able to answer the questions in these frames, he continues with the top frames. If he makes an error in this fast track, he goes down to the frames in the lower part of the page (the slow track), where the language is simpler and the questions are easier. The learner is free to change from one track to another depending upon his individual needs as he studies the programme.

Branching programme
A branching programme differs from the linear variety in the following ways:

1. The frame contains more information than a typical linear frame.
2. The question in the frame uses the multiple-choice format. The learner is required to select the correct answer from a number of possible answers.
3. The frame does not give the correct answer. Instead, each of the choices leads the learner to a different frame. If he chooses the correct answer, the frame presents new information. If he chooses any of the incorrect answers, the frame tells him why he is wrong. He is then sent back to the original frame to choose another answer.
4. The frames of a branching programme are arranged in a scrambled order. This arrangement prevents the learner from reading one frame after another without answering the questions.

The following figure shows the structure of a branching programme:

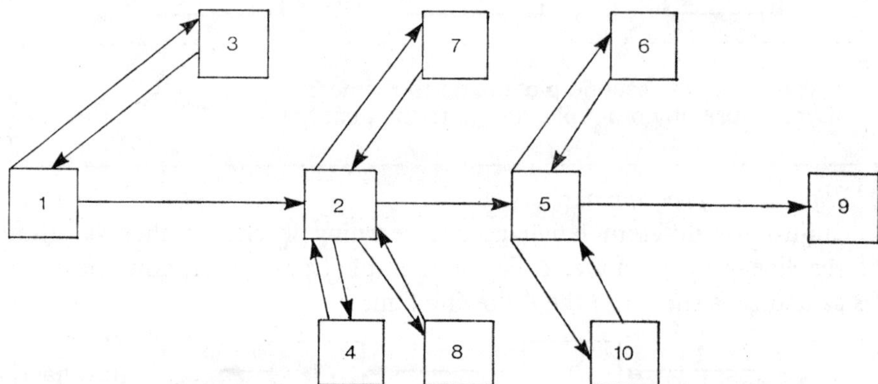

The learner goes through frames 1, 2, 5 and 9 if he makes no errors. All of these frames contain a new piece of information and a multiple-choice question. Frames 3, 4, 6, 7, 8 and 10 are called the remedial frames. Frame 3, for example, explains to the learner why his answer on Frame 1 is incorrect. It sends him back to the original frame to choose the correct answer. Frames 4, 7 and 8 help those learners who make three different types of errors on Frame 2. It is possible for the learner to make all these errors before choosing the correct answer. Figure 29 is an actual example of a branching programme. This segment teaches the learner how to use a ruler.

In this segment, Frame 3 is obviously a main frame. It gives two important rules for measuring with the ruler. In the multiple-choice question, the programmer has anticipated different kinds of misunderstandings. The first choice reveals a total misunderstanding. The second one is the correct answer. The third one is chosen by the learner who did not understand the rule about the zero end of the ruler. The last choice reveals a misunderstanding about the other end of the object. Notice that each of the remedial frames (Frames 4, 7 and 8) explains why the learner's choice is incorrect before sending him back for another try. Frame 5, which corresponds to the correct choice, congratulates the learner and presents a new piece of information.

Skip branching

Branching programmes clear up any misunderstanding on the part of the learner. But they use only one type of question. Many programmers believe that the learner learns more by writing his own answer instead of merely choosing the correct one.

FIGURE 29. *An example of a branching programme*

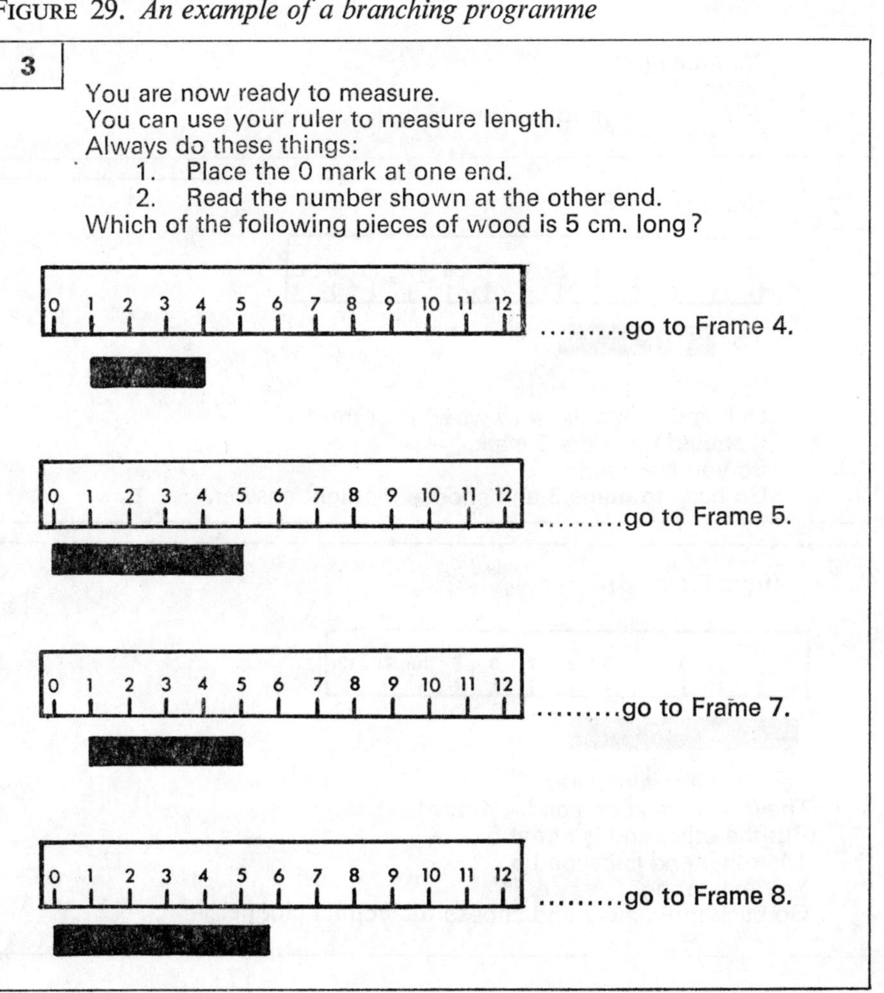

4 (from Frame 3)

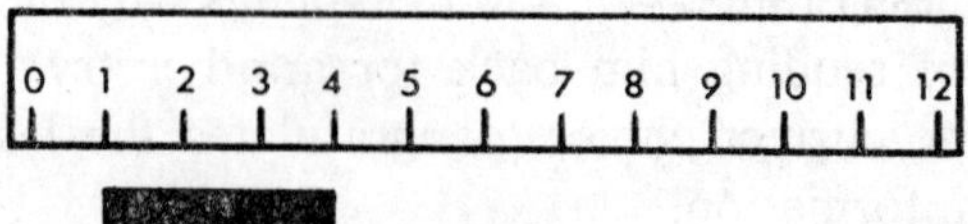

You chose this picture.
This is not correct.
The 0 mark is not at one end.
The other end is not 5.
Go back to Frame 3 and choose again.

5 (from Frame 3)

You are right!
Very good!
Now let's learn to measure by half cms.

7 (from Frame 3)

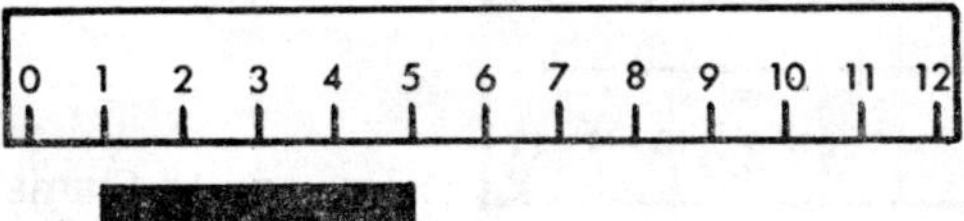

You chose this picture.
One end of the piece of wood is at the 1 mark.
It should be at the 0 mark.
So you are wrong.
Go back to frame 3 and choose the right answer.

8 (from Frame 3)

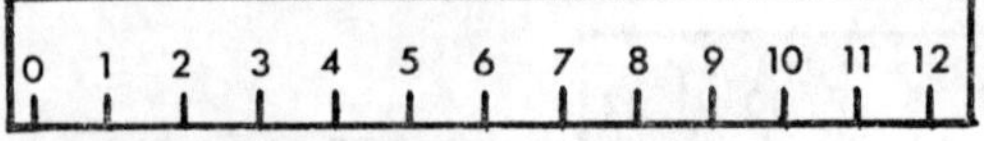

You chose this picture.
The 0 mark is at one end.   Good!
But the other end is not at 5.
The other end is beyond 5.
You are wrong.
Go back to Frame 3 and choose the correct picture.

A variation of the branching programme is called 'skip branching'. It has the advantage of both the branching programme and direct questions. The following figure is an explanation of its structure.

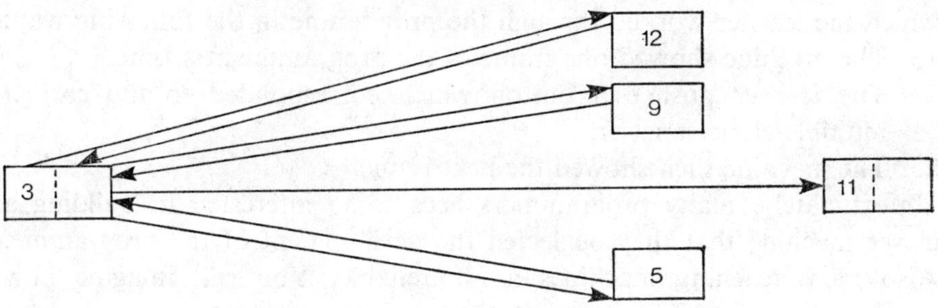

Frame 3 is one of the main frames. It is divided into two parts. The first part contains information and a direct question. After writing his answer, the learner goes to the second part of the frame. Instead of the correct answer, this part shows a list of possible answers and asks the learner to choose the one which is the same as his. For example, let us assume that the correct length is 4 cm. The second section may look like this:

> What answer did you get?
> If your answer was 6 cm., go to Frame 12.
> If your answer was 5 cm., go to Frame 9.
> If your answer was 4 cm., go to Frame 11.
> If your answer was different, go to Frame 5.

Depending upon the choice of the answer, the remedial frame will tell the learner what he did wrong: used the wrong end of the ruler, or began at the 1 cm. division instead of the zero. It will send him back for another try. Of course, it is impossible to anticipate all types of errors the learner may make. That is why the last choice is provided.

Adjunct programmes

This type of programme very closely resembles a workbook. The learner first reads a story. He is given a series of questions based on the story. After answering each question, he checks the correct answer. If he is wrong, he is told which page and line of the story he should read again for the correct answer.

Machines and media

In the early days of programmed instruction, there was a heavy emphasis on the use of 'teaching machines'. These machines controlled the way in which the learner worked through the programme in the following way:

1. The machine showed one frame of the programme at a time.
2. The learner pushed a button which corresponded to the correct multiple-choice answer.
3. The machine then showed the next frame.

Unfortunately, many programmers became so interested in building a clever machine that they neglected the development of the programme. Also most teaching machines are unreliable. You can imagine how confused a learner became when the machine refused to move or gave incorrect answers. In addition, teaching machines limited the programmer to frames of a specified size and questions which can be answered by pressing buttons.

Except for very young learners, teaching machines are unnecessary. However, there are other types of 'teaching machines' which programmers may find useful. These are such equipment as radio sets, film projectors and tape recorders. The principles and process of programming can be easily applied to these different media. Many programmes use radio, television and tape recordings in combination with printed materials.

Programmed tutoring

It is impossible to use a self-instructional programme with an illiterate. For one thing, the learner has to be taught how to use the material. For another, he may not be able to compare his answers with the correct answer. The combination of tutors and programmed instruction provides an effective solution to this problem. One thing a human tutor can do which no machine can do is to *listen to the learner*. This opens up many new opportunities for programmed instruction.

The best known programmed-tutoring system was created by Dr. Douglas Ellson. In this system, there are two major sections: the content programme and the operational programme. The former is similar to the frames of a linear programme while the latter is a series of instructions to the tutor. Figure 30 is a frame from a content programme, while Figure 31 is from an operational programme which accompanies the frame.

FIGURE 30. *A frame from a content programme*

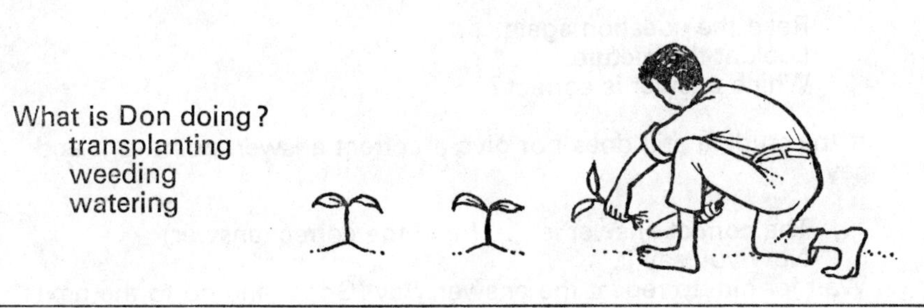

FIGURE 31. *An operational programme to accompany Figure* 30

HOW TO BEGIN:

Use a card to cover the multiple-choice answers under the question.

Show the frame to the student and say: 'Read the question and give me the answer'.

Wait for the student to respond.

CORRECT

If the student gives the correct answer, say 'Good' and go to the next frame.

INCORRECT

If the student gives an incorrect response, use the following prompts:

What does the question ask?
What is the answer?
Look at the picture.
Now give me the answer.
Read the question again.
Look at the picture.
Find the answer in the picture.
What is the answer from the picture?

If the student does not give a correct answer after these prompts, show the multiple-choice answers and say:

(Continued on the next page.)

> Look at these answers.
> Read the correct answer.
>
> Read the question again.
> Look at the picture.
> Which answer is correct?
>
> If the student still does not give a correct answer, point to it and say:
>
> The correct answer is . . . (read the correct answer).
> Now you say it.
> Wait for him to repeat the answer. Say 'Good' and go to the next frame.

The operational programme first tells the tutor how to begin the lesson. In this example, the tutor covers the answers and asks the learner to read the question. After reading the question, the learner may give a correct answer or an incorrect one. Each of these types of answer is followed by specific instructions. The learner is taken to the next frame if he gives the correct answer. In the case of an incorrect answer, the tutor uses a set of prompts: the learner is asked to read the question again; later he is asked to look at the picture; he is told to find the answer in the picture. If these prompts do not work, the tutor shows the learner three possible answers and asks him to choose one. Again he is helped with a series of prompts. Finally, if everything else fails, the tutor reads the correct answer and asks the learner to repeat it.

A unique aspect of programmed tutoring is the way in which prompts are used. As you can see, this is the opposite of the fading technique we discussed earlier. Instead of giving the strongest prompt at first and fading out gradually, the tutor gives as few prompts as possible. If the learner gives the correct answer anytime during the use of prompts, the sequence ends. Thus the learner receives as much—and only as much—help as he needs. This procedure is called 'reverse fading' or 'brightening' by Dr. Ellson. It permits the learner to discover the correct answer at his own level.

Programmed games

In recent years, programmers have designed teaching games for use by small groups of learners. These games use the basic principles of programmed instruction. At the same time, they permit learners to learn from each other. Here is a sample programmed game to teach word recognition:

Materials

This game uses fifty flashcards with a word on one side. Depending upon the level of the players, from five to ten different words are used. The same word appears on several cards. The word may be printed in different styles and sizes. A collection of pebbles is used for keeping score.

Number of players

Two to eight.

Preliminaries

1. Each player is given five pebbles. The remainder of the pebbles is set aside as the 'bank'.

2. The players select one of the words to be the key word.

Play

1. One player deals out the cards one by one, as far as they will go.

2. Each player picks up his cards without looking at them. He arranges them in a neat pile with the words facing down.

3. Beginning with the first player, players take turns flipping the top card of their pile and placing it face up in the middle.

4. If the turned-up card contains the key word, any player may place his hand upon it. The first player to do this gets a pebble from the bank.

5. If a player mistakenly places his hand on a card with some other word, he loses a pebble. This pebble goes to the bank.

6. The game ends when all cards have been turned up. The player with the most pebbles is the winner.

7. The game is repeated with a different key word.

This game uses many of the principles of programmed instruction. The task for the learner is to recognize a single word—a 'small step' of learning. There are also 'immediate results'. If the player places his hand on the key-word card, other players confirm it. If he makes an error, other players immediately point it out. The learner does *not* work at his own speed. But the game permits learning simple words first and then working with difficult ones. Once the player has mastered the rules of this game, he will be able to play any of the following variations:

Reading of sentences. Instead of using flashcards with words, the game may be played with sentences. The player may be asked to place his hand on one particular sentence. Later, he may be given cards with different sentences and asked to identify those sentences which are false. In this variation, knowledge of the subject matter as well as reading skills are involved.

TABLE 14. *Different types of programmes*

TYPE OF PROGRAMME	CHARACTERISTICS OF LEARNERS	SUBJECT MATTER
1. *Linear programme.* A self-instructional programme in which all learners use the same sequence. However, each learner works at his own speed.	All learners are at the same level.	The subject matter is easy and straightforward.
2. *Wash-back programmes.* This is a linear programme in which the test frames tell the learner to return to previous teaching frames if he makes an error. The learner is required to review these frames and try the test frame again.	Learners are at different ability levels.	Difficult subject matter in which mastery of early material is important for later work.
3. *Wash-ahead programme.* This is a linear programme which begins with a test frame. Those who answer this frame skip a set of teaching frames and proceed directly to the next unit.	Learners are at different levels.	Important skills are needed for learning the subject matter.
4. *Multiple-track programme.* The fast track consists of a series of difficult frames. The learner has the option of dropping down to a set of easier frames dealing with the same subject matter.	Learners are at different ability levels. Also suitable for a community in which some learners have a high level of literacy skills and others have a low level.	Transition from small-step programmes to larger reading exercises.
5. *Branching programme.* The frames of this programme are large. They include a multiple-choice question.	Learners have the ability to follow directions.	The subject matter emphasizes reading comprehension and plays down writing skills.
6. *Adjunct programme.* The learner is required to read a story and answer a series of questions. Correct answers and page references are provided.	Learners have the ability to read at high level and follow directions.	The subject matter emphasizes reading comprehension and plays down writing skills.
7. *Media programme.* In this type of programme one part is provided by a booklet, poster, filmstrip or television. Another part is provided by a tape recording, radio broadcast or television broadcast.	Beginning learners.	Literacy skills where oral instructions are needed. Also suited for establishing the link between the spoken and the printed word.
8. *Programmed tutoring.* A tutor presents frames to the learner. The amount of help from the tutor depends upon the learner's response.	Beginning learners.	The subject matter emphasizes oral reading.
9. *Programmed games.* Games which do not require the presence of a teacher.	A group of students at different entry levels who are willing to learn from each other.	Basic tasks which require repeated drill practice.

Spelling. This variation is played with a set of flashcards with letters. A key word is identified at the beginning of the game. Players watch out for the first letter of the word. After this letter is identified by a player, he is given a pebble and the letter is placed on a stand. The players now look for the second letter. The game continues in this fashion until all the letters for the word are identified in the correct sequence.

Choosing the best type of programme

Which type of programme is the best one? There is no one best type of programme to suit all occasions. It has to be chosen on the basis of a number of factors.

Table 14 summarizes the characteristics of different types of programmes. The table also indicates different characteristics of learners and different types of subject matter which are best served by each format.

Learner characteristics and the type of programme

In general, the choice of the type of programme depends upon the type of answers which the learner can give. At the beginning level, when the learner is limited to spoken answers, programmed tutoring and programmed games are highly recommended. Later, as the learner is able to select the correct answer by pointing, underlining, circling or drawing lines, he can move to simple linear programmes with selection-type questions. When the learner is capable of writing, he uses a regular linear programme or an adjunct programme.

Learner preferences also determine the type of programme. In some communities, the use of games may be considered unsuitable for learning. If the learners are at different levels, we should make use of this opportunity to have them learn from each other. A positive attitude towards such media as radio and television is also an important consideration in the choice of the type of programme.

Literacy skills and the type of programme

Table 15 lists various literacy skills and indicates the most suitable type of programme for each skill.

Local resources and the type of programme

The initial selection of the type of programme is made on the basis of learner characteristics, subject matter and literacy skills. However, the final choice has to be made on the basis of local resources. If we do not have the appropriate equipment, any type of media programming is beyond our capabilities. The absence of a good artist rules out non-verbal approaches. Programmed tutoring requires a large number of volunteer workers who have the motivation and the ability to follow directions. If the learners are dispersed over a wide rural area, a self-instructional programme is needed. On the other hand, in a factory situation where time and space for literacy efforts are donated by the management, media programmes can be effectively used.

TABLE 15. *Different literacy skills and types of programmes*

LITERACY SKILL	PREFERRED PROGRAMME FORMAT
1. Make associations between the spoken and the printed words.	Programmed tutoring and programmed games.
2. Interpret pictures.	Programmed tutoring, programmed games, and linear programmes with a non-verbal emphasis.
3. Follow spoken directions.	Audiovisual programmes, programmed tutoring and programmed games.
4. Use writing materials properly.	Linear programmes with pictures.
5. Trace letters and words.	Wash-back and wash-ahead sequences in which the teacher decides whether the learner's writing meets acceptable standards.
6. Count.	Audiovisual programmes, programmed tutoring and programmed games.
7. Recognize numerals.	Audiovisual programmes, programmed tutoring, programmed games, and linear programmes which require the learner to match numerals and sets of objects.
8. Sight read a small number of words.	Audiovisual programmes and programmed tutoring.
9. Sound out new words in context.	Programmed tutoring and programmed games.
10. Read words and sentences aloud.	Programmed tutoring.
11. Demonstrate literal comprehension.	Programmed tutoring with spoken responses.
12. Copy familiar words.	Wash-back and wash-ahead sequences in which the teacher determines if the learner's writing has reached acceptable standards.
13. Form and write words.	Linear programmes which require simple written responses.
14. Perform simple addition and subtraction. Use simple fractions.	Linear programmes, programmed tutoring and skip branching programmes. Programmed games for drill practice.
15. Sight read extensive sets of words.	Linear and branching programmes.
16. Read silently and demonstrate comprehension of the material.	Branching, adjunct and multiple-track programmes.
17. Demonstrate ability to understand implied meanings.	Branching programmes.
18. Form and write words and short sentences.	Linear and adjunct programmes with frequent written responses.
19. Write short notes.	Linear programmes dealing with writing.
20. Perform simple multiplication and division.	Linear programmes to introduce basic rules. Branching and skip branching programmes to diagnose errors and to provide remedial instruction. Programmed games to provide drill practice.

Summary

In this chapter we discussed a variety of ways in which the principles and the process of programming can be used. The linear programme can be made more useful by using the wash-back, wash-ahead and multiple-track varieties. Branching and adjunct programmes serve different useful purposes. A programme may be presented through a teaching machine and in a variety of media. Programmed tutoring helps a tutor produce effective results with an illiterate learner. In contrast to self-instructional programmes, there are programmed games which involve a group of learners. These games encourage learners to help each other in their learning activities.

The choice of a suitable type of programme is based on: (a) the characteristics of the learner; (b) the subject matter; (c) literacy skills; and (d) the local resources. Each type of programme has its own advantages and limitations.

We have already discussed the production of linear programmes in Chapter 5. While the same principles of programming apply to different types, specific production techniques may differ. Chapter 8 deals with the preparation of programmed tutoring materials and Chapter 9 deals with the construction of programmed games.

PRACTICAL EXERCISE

1. *Study the programme you have prepared earlier and see if a part of it can be improved by using any other format. If so, rewrite the programme using a different format.*

CHAPTER EIGHT

How to prepare programmed-tutoring materials

This chapter deals with the preparation of programmed-tutoring materials. As we saw in an earlier chapter, these types of materials are especially suitable for training volunteers to tutor illiterate learners.

Different parts of programmed-tutoring materials

A set of programmed-tutoring materials consists of a 'content' programme and an 'operational' programme. The adult learner uses the content programme while the tutor follows instructions from the operational programme.

Here is another example of programmed-tutoring materials. Before beginning the lesson the tutor gets a copy of the content programme and the operational programme for the next lesson.

The content programme

Let us imagine that the content programme deals with the subject matter of transplanting thakalis and with the literacy skills of reading and answering a question. Some examples of frames are shown in Figure 32. All frames of this lesson have the same format: a picture, a question and three multiple-choice answers.

The pictures show seedlings ready for transplantation, digging up the seedlings and replanting. Some questions ask for facts: 'How many leaves does this plant have?' Other questions require an inference: 'Will the farmer transplant this thakali?' Still others require an opinion: 'How does the farmer feel?' Finally, there are some questions which require problem solving: 'How can the farmer stop stepping on the plants?'

FIGURE 32. *Examples of frames from the content programme*

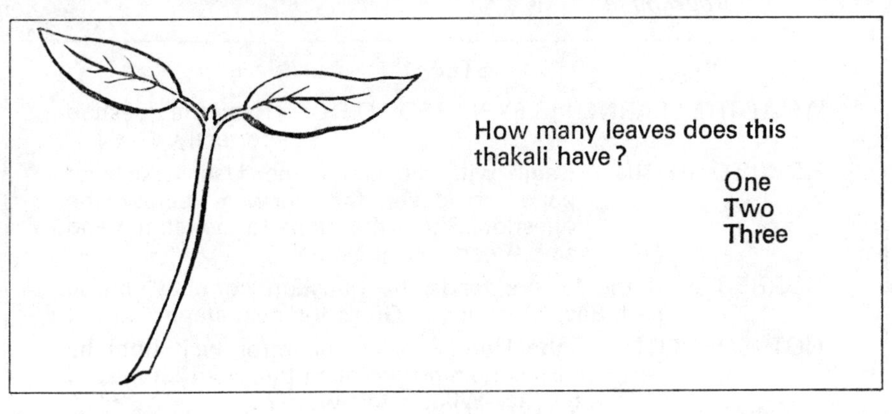

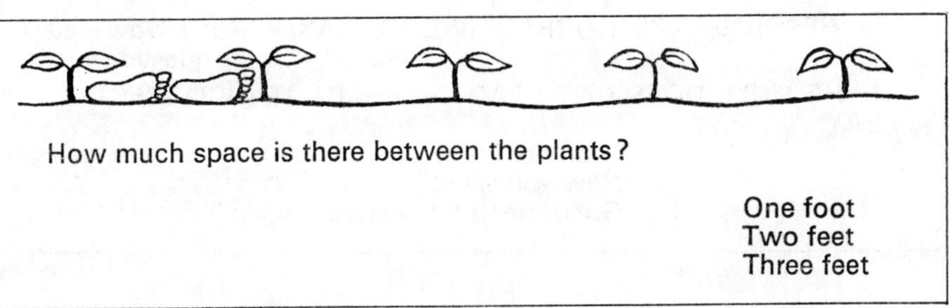

The operational programme
The operational programme for this lesson is shown in Figure 33.

Progress sheets
During each tutoring lesson, the tutor fills out a progress sheet (Figure 34). This sheet tells the tutor which frames to repeat during the next lesson. The tutor records a symbol √ for those frames which the learner answers correctly on the first step. Frames in which the learner makes a mistake are marked with an X. As you can see from the first row in Figure 34, this learner missed Frames 1, 7 and 9 during his first attempt. In the next lesson, the tutor took the learner through only these frames. During each new tutoring lesson the learner works through only those frames he missed in the previous lesson. As you can see on the chart, he misses the ninth Frame during the second lesson and again during the next one. Finally, in the fourth lesson he gives the correct answer. In the next lesson the tutor presents *all* the frames once again. As you can see from the figure, the learner answers all frames correctly. If he misses any frames the same procedure will be repeated again.

FIGURE 33. *Three steps for question comprehension from the operational programme*

STEP 1

WHAT THE LEARNER IS EXPECTED TO DO: Read the question correctly.

HOW TO BEGIN: Begin with the first frame. Use a piece of paper to cover the answers below the question. Show the frame to the learner and say, 'Read the question'.

CORRECT: If the learner reads the question correctly, praise him. Say, 'Very good'. Go to the next step.

NOT CORRECT: If the learner makes an error wait until he finishes reading. Point to the word he missed and say, 'What is this word?'.

IF HE GIVES THE CORRECT WORD, SAY: 'Good. Now read the question again.'

IF HE STILL DOES NOT READ OR READS IT INCORRECTLY, SAY:

'That word is . . . .'
'Now you say it.'
'Good. Read the question again.'

STEP 2

WHAT THE LEARNER IS EXPECTED TO DO: Answer the question using information from the picture.

HOW TO BEGIN: After the learner completes reading the question, pause to see if he gives the answer himself. If not, say, 'Now give me the answer to the question'.

CORRECT: If he gives an acceptable answer to the question using information from the picture, praise the learner and go to the next step. The learner's answer need not be the same as the correct answer given below the question.

NOT CORRECT: If he does not give any answer or gives an incorrect answer, use the following prompts— one at a time. When he does give the correct answer, go to CORRECT.

PROMPTS: Read the question again. What is the answer?
Read the question again. Look at the picture.
What is the answer?
Look at the picture. Find the answer to the question in the picture.
The answer is . . . . Now you say it.

STEP 3

WHAT THE LEARNER IS EXPECTED TO DO: The learner chooses the best of three possible answers to the question and reads it aloud.

HOW TO BEGIN: Remove the piece of paper covering the three possible answers. Show them to the learner and say, 'Which one of these is the correct answer? Read it to me'.

CORRECT: If the learner reads the correct answer, praise him. Go to the next frame.

PARTLY CORRECT: If the learner points to the correct answer but does not read it, say, 'That's right. Now read it to me'.

If the learner reads it correctly, go to CORRECT.
If the learner does not read it or reads it incorrectly, go to NOT CORRECT.

NOT CORRECT: If the learner does not read the answer, or reads the incorrect answer, use the following prompts—one by one. Whenever he gives the correct answer, go to CORRECT.

PROMPTS: Read the question. Which one of these is the correct answer to the question?
Look at the picture. Read the correct answer.
Read the question. Look at the picture. Now which answer is the correct one?
This is the correct answer (point to it). Read it to me.
This is the correct answer. It says . . . now you read it.

General procedure for producing programmed-tutoring materials

Given below are different steps in the production of programmed-tutoring materials. Each step is then described in detail.

1. Select a suitable literacy skill.
2. Write frames for the content programme.
3. Develop a suitable tutoring method.
4. Write the operational programme.
5. Produce the complete set of materials.

FIGURE 34. *Sample progress sheet for programmed tutoring*

Frames	Lessons					
	1	2	3	4	5	6
1	✗	✓	✓	✓	✓	
2	✓				✓	
3	✓				✓	
4	✓				✓	
5	✓	✓	✓	✓	✓	
6	✓				✓	
7	✗				✓	
8	✓				✓	
9	✗	✗	✗	✓	✓	
10	✓				✓	

Selecting a suitable literacy skill
Based on the literacy-skills analysis, we select the major skill for a programmed-tutoring lesson. In the beginning we may concentrate on sight-reading skills. Later we may introduce various word-attack and comprehension skills.

Writing the content programme
Writing the content programme uses the same principles as writing a linear programme. Programmed tutoring requires that all frames of a lesson have the same format. This permits the tutor to use the same method of teaching. The frames from the earlier example on transplanting thakali all have the same format: a picture showing some important activity in the transplanting procedure, a question dealing with an idea illustrated in the picture and a set of three possible answers. The sequence of this lesson is the same as the sequence of transplanting.

Developing a tutoring method
Once the frames for a lesson are written, the programmer plans the tutoring method. He uses the basic principles of programmed instruction in this step. He may also actually tutor some learners from the community to see if his method is useful.

In the lesson on transplanting thakalis, the programmer began by asking the learner to read the question *and* give the correct answer. He found out that this step was too large. The learners took some time to read the question and in the end they forgot that they were also supposed to give an answer. So the programmer divided this step into the two steps of (1) reading the question and (2) giving the answer. The programmer had originally made the learner choose the correct answer from the multiple-choice statements. Later he decided to cover them up and get the learner's own answer first.

Writing the operational programme
We now translate our tutoring method into a set of instructions for the tutor. There instructions should be simple enough so that an untrained tutor can follow them.

In each step of the operational programme we explain how to begin. Then we list different types of answers from the learner. Finally, we tell the tutor what to do about each type of answer.

Presenting the frame. Before presenting the frame, the tutor may have to make some preliminary arrangements. In our examples, he has to cover the multiple-choice answers. These instructions are given under the heading 'How to begin'.

Listing and classifying answers. At this stage we anticipate different answers that the learner is likely to give. Basically, all learners' answers may be classified into the major types listed in Table 16.

TABLE 16. *Different types of learners' answer in programmed tutoring*

TYPE OF ANSWER	EXAMPLES
1. Correct answer	The learner is asked to read a question. He reads the entire question correctly. The learner is asked to say the sum. He says the correct sum.
2. Incorrect answer	The learner is asked to read a question. He omits an important word. The learner is asked to say the sum of 3+2. He says, 'Six'.
3. No answer	The learner is asked to read a question. He remains silent. The learner is asked to say the sum. He remains silent.
4. Unclear answer	The learner is asked to read a question. He reads it in a soft voice. You do not know if his response is correct or not. The learner is asked to say the sum. You do not hear his answer clearly.
5. Partly correct answer	The learner is asked to read the correct answer from three possible answers. The learner points to the correct answer but does not read it. The learner is asked to count the total number of objects in two pictures. He counts the number of objects in the first one and stops.
6. More-than-correct answer	The learner is asked to read a question. He not only reads the question but also gives the correct answer.

Types of answers to a frame. A brief statement of each type of answer is given in the operational programme under such headings as 'Correct', 'Not correct', and 'Partly correct'.

Tutor's response to each type of answer. At this stage we systematically go through each type of answer and tell the tutor exactly what to do about it. We need not write separate instructions for each type of answer listed in Table 16. Very often the no-answer category is combined with the incorrect-answer category. Instructions for handling each type of answer are listed in Table 17.

TABLE 17. *Tutoring instructions for different types of answers*

TYPE OF ANSWER		SUITABLE INSTRUCTIONS
1.	Correct answer	Praise the learner and go to the next step.
2.	Incorrect answer and no answer	Do not criticize the learner. Do not call his attention to the error. Give him prompt 5. (More details on prompting are given below.)
3.	Unclear answer	Do not criticize the learner. Say, 'Read that again for me' or 'What did you say? Repeat that for me'.
4.	Partly-correct answer	Praise the learner for what he has done correctly and ask him to continue. For example, say, 'That's good. Continue counting with the other picture'.
5.	More-than-correct answer	Praise the learner. Skip the step he has already completed.

Praise, punishment, prompting and brightening

At this stage we would like to discuss some underlying principles of programmed tutoring. One of these is the use of praise. As you can see from Table 17 above, the learner is praised for every correct response he makes. Such praise encourages him to make more correct responses. We carefully avoid any form of punishment or criticism. It is important for the tutor not to lose his or her patience. If the learner makes an error, the tutor immediately provides prompts to help him.

When the learner makes a mistake, we simplify the task. This is what we do when we ask the learner to count if he is not able to add. We also remind the learner of various things he should be using; if he is unable to answer the question, we ask him to read the question again with the hope he will understand it this time. We also ask him to look at the picture where information for the correct answer is to be found. The prompts are arranged in a 'brightening' sequence: we begin with the task in its most difficult level and gradually add more and more prompts. In the end we tell the learner the correct answer and ask him to repeat it. However, if the learner is able to give the correct answer anywhere in the sequence, prompting stops and the learner is taken to the next step.

Producing a complete set of tutoring materials

So far we have dealt with the preparation of one programmed-tutoring lesson. A number of different types of lessons make up a complete set. For example, in teaching the transplanting of thakalis we may want to begin with another lesson which gives more information and teaches the learner another aspect of reading comprehension. We have to prepare a new lesson with a new type of frame and a new operational programme for sentence comprehension. Earlier lessons in this series may teach the learner to sight-read a basic set of words and apply word-attack skills to similar-sounding words. To prepare the complete set, all these different lessons and operational programmes should be combined.

Trying out programmed-tutoring materials

The testing of programmed-tutoring materials is divided into three phases: (a) testing the content programme; (b) testing the operational programme; and (c) testing the complete programme. Here are some practical suggestions for each of these phases.

Testing the content programme

1. Using the first version of the content programme, tutor a learner and make suitable revisions of the content materials. Do not make changes in the operational programme at this stage.
2. Test the material with a new learner. Repeat this testing and revision procedure with four or five individual learners.

Testing the operational programme

3. Change your operational programme to suit the revised set of frames. Try it out with some more individual learners. Make suitable revisions whenever necessary.
4. Simplify the steps and prompts in the operational programme until you have the simplest possible version.

Testing the entire package

5. Find a tutor, provide him with the content and operational programmes and ask him to tutor *you*. Play the role of a slow learner and make all possible types of errors. Revise the operational programme on the basis of the tutor's performance and his suggestions.

6. Watch the tutor as he works with an actual learner. Do not interfere, but take notes on a duplicate set. At the end of the tutoring session, inspect the learner's progress sheet and interview both the tutor and the learner.

7. Test the entire package with a new tutor and a new learner over a long period of time. Make final revisions on the basis of suggestions from the tutor and the student.

Other types of programmed-tutoring lessons

The following table (Table 18) outlines some other types of programmed-tutoring lesson.

TABLE 18. *Types of programmed-tutoring lessons*

LITERACY SKILL	CONTENT PROGRAMME	OPERATIONAL PROGRAMME
Sight reading	Frames with a sentence, phrase, word, syllable or letter.	Ask the learner to read the frame. If he fails, read it for him and ask him to repeat it.
Free reading	Frames with complete paragraphs or stories.	Ask the learner to read. Let him continue reading until he makes a major mistake. Read the word for him and ask him to repeat it. After completing the frame, ask him to read the sentence again.
Contextual word-attack	Frame with an incomplete sentence. The sentence has a strong context.	Ask the learner to read the sentence and fill in the blank. If he fails, prompt by having him re-read the incomplete sentence. Provide multiple-choice answers and ask him to read the best-fitting word to complete the sentence.
	Frame with a sentence containing a new word in a strong context.	Ask the learner to read the sentence. If he cannot read the new word, let him complete reading the sentence and try again. Provide a choice of answers and let him select the best word.
Phonetic word-attack	Frame with a single new word. This word contains familiar letters or syllables.	Ask the learner to read the word. If he fails, point to each phonetic element (letter or syllable) and ask, 'What sound does this make?'. Point to larger parts of the word and have learner sound them until he can sound the entire word.
Instruction comprehension	Frame with a command involving real objects (e.g., 'Pick up the ruler.') or pictures (e.g., 'Point to the ruler in the picture.').	Ask the learner to read the sentence. Then ask him to do what it says. If he fails, ask him to read the sentence again and do what it says. Demonstrate the action and ask the learner to imitate you.
Sentence comprehension	Frame with one or two sentences followed by a question on their meaning.	Ask the learner to read one sentence at a time. Correct any errors. Then ask him to read the question. If he does not provide an answer, ask him for one. Prompt by referring back to the sentences.

(Continued on the next page.)

| Story comprehension | One frame contains a complete story. Later frames contain individual questions on the content of the story. | Ask the learner to read the story. Correct major errors. Ask him to read one question at a time. If he does not provide an answer, ask for one. Prompt by pointing to the location in the story where the information is found. Ask the learner to read that part and answer the question. |

Variations in programmed tutoring

With newly literate tutors we may use the variation of programmed tutoring shown in Figure 35. In this type there are no operational programmes. Instead, instructions to the tutor are given on one side of the frame itself. The frame may be on a flashcard which the tutor holds up

FIGURE 35. *A variation of programmed tutoring*

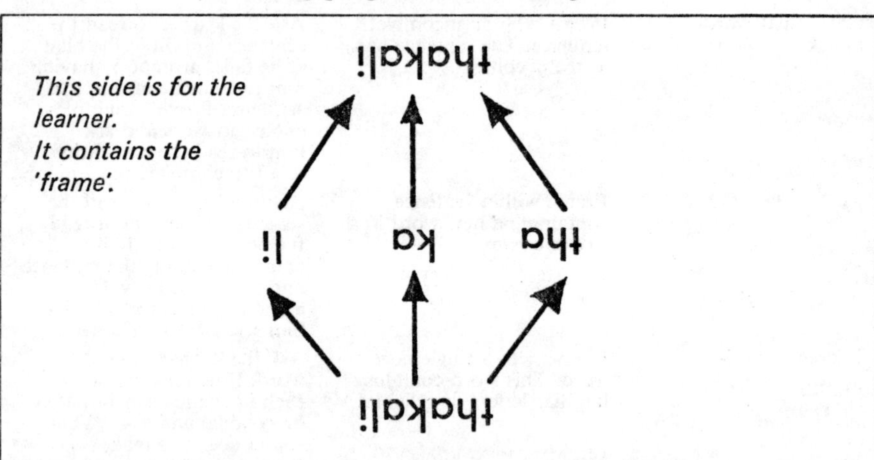

1. Point to the first word. Read the word slowly. Read it three times.
2. Ask the learner to read the word. Listen carefully. If he makes a mistake show him how to read it. If he reads correctly, say, 'Good'.
3. Point to 'tha'. Ask him what sound it makes. If he makes a mistake show him what sound it makes. If he is correct, say, 'Good'.
4. Do the same thing with 'ka' and 'li'.
5. Ask him to read the whole word. If he makes a mistake tell him how each part sounds. When he reads correctly, say, 'That's right'.
6. Go to the next frame.

This side faces the tutor. It contains instructions for him.

to the learner to let him see a word he is supposed to read. Instructions to the tutor are given on the other side of the card. The format illustrated in Figure 35 shows the frame for the learner at the top of the page and the instructions to the tutor on the bottom half of the page.

Summary

Programmed-tutoring materials consist of a content programme and an operational programme. The content programme contains about ten to twenty frames of the same type. The operational programme has sets of instructions to the tutor on how to present each frame and how to praise and prompt the learner.

In producing a programmed tutoring system, a suitable literacy skill is selected. A number of frames are written to focus on this literacy skill within the context of a selected subject matter. The frames are arranged in a logical sequence. The programmer designs a tutoring strategy using the basic principles of programmed instruction. He revises this strategy by trying it out with learners from the target group. Instructions to the tutor explain how to begin the step, what types of answers to expect and how to handle each type of answer. In general, the tutoring procedure avoids any criticism of the learner and uses praise for all his correct answers.

PRACTICAL EXERCISE

Return to your learner analysis at the end of Chapter 2. If you think that the programmed-tutoring format will be appropriate for this community, design suitable materials, using the following steps:
1. *Select a suitable literacy skill.*
2. *Write frames for the content programme.*
3. *Develop a suitable tutoring method.*
4. *Write the operational programme.*
5. *Produce the complete set of materials.*

CHAPTER NINE

How to prepare programmed games

This chapter discusses the preparation of programmed games for adult learners. These games are especially useful in teaching literacy skills.

Some general considerations

A 'programmed' game has rules for the play just like any other game. It is designed to help learners master specific skills. The game uses the basic principles of programmed instruction: players actively answer questions. The game uses small learning tasks. It provides the correct answer for each question. The game begins with easy activities and gradually becomes more difficult.

Procedure for preparing a programmed game

Here are the steps in preparing a programmed game:
1. Specify the literacy skill to be attained by the players of the game. This skill is based on the literacy skills-analysis.
2. Specify what the learners already know.
3. Choose a suitable type of game (e.g., a card game, a board game or some other local game).
4. Prepare game materials. These include flashcards, picture cards, scoring sheets, dice and gameboards.
5. Write the rules for the game. Make sure that playing the game involves suitable learning activities.
6. Revise the game to make it more interesting and effective.

An example of preparing a programmed game

Here is the description of an actual game-design project to show how the procedure is applied:

1. The programmer noticed that many of the adult learners had difficulty in discriminating between the words 'his' and 'her'. He decided to prepare a programmed game to help learners attain these two skills: (a) recognize the words 'his' and 'her' in print form; (b) associate the word 'his' with the masculine and 'her' with the feminine gender.

2. The learners already knew how to read twenty words. These words included different colour names and objects around the house.

3. The programmer chose card games because adults in his class enjoyed playing cards. He also decided to use a pair of dice.

4. The materials for the game consisted of twelve flashcards with a sentence on each. Six of the sentences began with the word 'his' and the other six with the word 'her'. The sentences were simple ones like 'His pencil is red' and 'Her book is blue'. The game also used two wooden cubes. One of the cubes contained the words 'his' and 'her' on three sides each. The other cube had six different nouns on each of the six faces. These were the nouns used in the sentence cards.

5. This is how the game was played. All twelve cards were placed on the floor with their sentence sides facing up. Players took turns to roll the two wooden cubes. The word 'his' or 'her' turned up on one cube and a noun turned up on the other. Players tried to find the card which contained both the pronoun and the noun. For example, if one cube showed 'her' and the other cube showed 'pen', the sentence card which contained both these words was 'Her pen is black'. The player to take this card won the round. Other players checked the card to make sure it had the correct words. The game continued with each player taking his turn to throw the cubes and all players trying to be the first to take the card. The game ended when all cards were taken. The player with the most cards was the winner.

   So far, the game trained the learners to see the difference between the words 'his' and 'her'. There was a second part to the game which trained them to associate 'his' with men and 'her' with women. In this part, the same two cubes were used, but the sentence cards were replaced by picture cards: six cards showing pictures of men with objects from the noun cube and six other cards with pictures of women with the same objects. The game was played exactly as in the first part except that players took picture cards instead of sentence cards.

6. The programmer checked the game for the use of programming principles. There were small steps which proceeded from easy tasks (matching words with words) to more complex ones (matching words with pictures). There were also frequent answers when players took the cards. The correct answer was given when they checked to see if the cards matched the words on the two cubes.

In revising a programmed game, the following questions are useful: (a) are the rules of the game simple? (b) are the rules related to literacy skills? (c) do the rules give all players an equal chance?; (d) is each round of the game brief? and (e) does the game combine chance and skill?

Using these questions, the programmer revised the game in a number of ways. The rules of the game were simple. Winning the game was related to literacy skills. In the first part of the game the learner had to discriminate between the words 'his' and 'her'. The second part required the learner to match these two words with the correct gender. Near the end of this game there were long periods of waiting because the words on the cubes did not match the remaining cards on the floor. To reduce this problem, the programmer made the following changes:

1. Instead of removing the card, the players were told to merely touch it. The first person to do so was given a pebble. The card was *not* removed. It was used in the game whenever the same two words turned up again.

2. The programmer replaced one 'his' and one 'her' on the cube with the combination 'his/her'. When this side turned up, the players were permitted to touch the picture of either a man or a woman.

3. The two parts of the game were combined into a single game. The cards had the sentences on one side and the pictures on the other. At the beginning of the game, the cards were placed with the sentence side up. Whenever a player touched a card, it was turned over to reveal the picture side. The next time the same two words turned up, the players had to touch the picture card. Thus the game began with sentences and ended up with pictures.

Although all players had an opportunity to participate during each round of the game, slower readers had problems competing with faster ones. As a result, they dropped out of the game. To reduce this problem, the programmer made these revisions:

1. The programmer replaced one of the words on the cube with a star. If this side turned up, only the player who threw the cubes during that round could touch a card. He might take as much time as he needed but he had to touch a card which went with the word 'his' or 'her' on the other cube.

2. There was a penalty for a player touching an incorrect card. This player lost a point and had to return one of his pebbles.

The programmer made some additional changes in the game. A description of the revised game is given below:

Materials and equipment

1. Twelve flashcards with sentences on one side and corresponding pictures on the other side. Six of the sentences begin with the word 'his' and the other six with 'her'. The sentences use six nouns already in the player's sight vocabulary.

2. Two wooden cubes with words pasted on them. One cube has five different nouns (e.g., pen, book, pencil, etc.) and a star. The other cube has the word 'his' on two sides, 'her' on two other sides, and the combination 'his/her' on the remaining two sides.

3. A small pile of pebbles.

Rules

1. All cards are placed in the middle of the play area with the sentence sides up.
2. The first player rolls both the cubes. All players see the 'his' or 'her' on one cube and the noun on the other cube.
3. The player who touches the card with the sentence which contains both the words scores a point. He takes a pebble from the centre.
4. If a player touches an incorrect card, he loses a point. He returns a pebble to the centre.
5. If the 'his/her' combination turns up, a player can place his hand on a sentence which has either word.
6. If the star turns up, only the player who threw the cubes can play that round. He has to touch any card which corresponds to the 'his' or 'her' on the other cube.
7. Game ends whenever a player collects ten pebbles. This player is the winner.
8. The game is played again with a change. At the beginning of the game, the cards are shuffled and six cards are dealt picture side up, the other six sentence side up. The players now touch the sentences or pictures which correspond to the words on the cubes.

Trying out programmes

Programmed games are tried out in two stages. First you play the game with your friends, then you play it with a group of learners. Here are some practical suggestions for these try-outs:

1. Use a small group of three to five players. This permits you to observe everyone during the game.
2. Get the group playing the game as soon as possible. Do not spend too much time explaining all the rules. Start off with only the essential rules; you may explain the other rules later, if and when the need arises.
3. Take part in the play of the game so that the learners do not see you as an outsider. At the same time, do not dominate the game.
4. Help players only if a serious problem stops the game. Very often players themselves come up with suitable rules to handle unexpected events.
5. Listen carefully to players' comments. This helps you to identify confusing parts of the game.

6.   At the end of the game ask the learners how they felt while playing
and what they learned. You can give them an informal test.

The most important thing in making changes in a game is to balance
instruction and motivation. Too much fun without any learning, and
mechanical learning without any fun, are both to be avoided. Simplify all
rules which confuse the learner. Remove unnecessary rules which are
rarely used.

Adapting a programmed game

A useful short-cut in designing a programmed game is to take a popular
game and change it to teach new skills. In Chapter 7 we described a
word-recognition game and showed how it can be adapted to teach
sentence reading and spelling. Let us take the game described above and
use it to teach two other skills.

Simple addition

This variation is designed to teach basic numeracy skills. In this game,
there are twelve cards, each with a picture on one side and a number on
the other. The picture side has two rows of objects. For example, it may
have pictures of three cows on the top row and four more cows on the
bottom. The number on the other side of our example card is seven. The
game also uses two cubes, one with the numbers 0, 1, 2, 3, 4 and 5, and
the other with the numbers 6, 7, 8, 9 and 10. The second cube also has a
star which stands for any number the player chooses. A small collection
of pebbles is used for keeping score.

This 'addition' game is played just like the previous game. Play begins
with the cards spread out on the floor with their picture sides up. One
player throws the two cubes. Two different numbers turn up. The first
player to touch the picture with the corresponding number of objects wins
a point. In later stages of the game, players try to touch the card showing
the number which is the sum.

Spelling

This variation is designed to give practice in recognizing various combina-
tions of consonants and vowels. There are twelve cards each with a single
syllable word on one side (e.g., cat, bed, lip, pot, tub) and a picture on
the other. One of the cubes has a different consonant on each face and
the other cube has five different vowels and a star.

The rules for this game are very similar to those for the previous game. One player rolls the cubes. Two letters turn up—one a consonant and the other a vowel. The first player to place his hand upon the card which has the word with the particular consonant-vowel combination scores a point. In later stages of the game, players read the letters on the cubes and identify the appropriate picture.

Adapting popular games for instruction

Adults in the community often have popular traditional games. Many of these can be adapted for teaching literacy and numeracy skills.

Figure 36 is an example of this type of adaptation. It shows the board for a game played by the women in a rural community during their spare hours. There are a hundred spaces in the board and each player begins with his pebble on the first space. The first player to move his pebble to the hundredth square wins the game. The number of squares to be moved during each round is determined by throwing six coins. The number of heads turning up indicates how many spaces to move. The snakes and ladders on the board make the game more exciting. If a player's pebble ends in a space with a ladder, he 'climbs' the ladder and places his pebble in another space at a higher level. For example, the person who lands on the fourth space immediately goes to the twenty-sixth space. On the other hand, if a person comes to a space with the mouth of the snake, he gets swallowed' by the snake and takes his pebble to the lower level where the snake's tail ends. For example, the person who lands on the thirty-fifth space comes down to the eighteenth space.

The key element in this game is the way players move across the board. Instead of tossing coins, we can use a packet of flashcards with numbers on one side. Each player takes a card and moves the number of spaces indicated. This provides practice in reading numbers. Players may also be asked to take two cards, add the numbers together and use the total to move their pebbles. We can also have the players pick two cards, find the difference between them (this gives them practice in subtraction). We can even allow the player to decide whether he wants to add or subtract so that he can get to a square with a ladder or avoid one with a snake.

Another way in which this game can be adapted for instructional purposes is to use cards with questions on them. The player chooses a card, reads the question on it and gives an answer. Other players check his answer by comparing it with the correct answer found on the back of the card. If correct, the player moves the appropriate number of spaces depending upon the difficulty level of the question.

FIGURE 36. *Snakes and ladders game board*

More programmed games

Descriptions of four more programmed games are given below. All of these games are adaptations of popular games. We have also given examples of how each game is modified to teach other skills.

CONCENTRATION

Purpose of the game: To provide practice in sight-reading.
Materials: A number of flashcards, some with pictures and others with words. For each picture card there is a corresponding word card. About ten cards with pictures and ten with words are needed for the game.
Number of players: Two to five.
Approximate time requirement: Five to ten minutes. The game can be replayed any number of times.

Play:

1. One player shuffles all cards and spreads them on the floor with their faces down. The cards do not have to be arranged in neat rows and columns, but they should not touch each other.

2. The first player turns any two cards face up so that all players see what is on them. These cards remain face up on the floor in the same location.

3. If the two cards match (e.g., if one of them has a picture of a spade and the other the word 'spade'), the player takes them for his collection. He also gets another chance to turn over two more cards.

4. If the cards do not match (e.g., if both cards have pictures, or if both have words, or if one has a picture which does not match the word on the other), they are turned face down in the same place.

5. The game continues with each player turning over any two cards. Players try to remember the positions of cards turned up earlier. All matching cards are collected by the players who turned them face up. The game ends when all cards have been collected by different players. The player with the most cards wins the game.

Variations: The basic element in this game is the matching of two different cards. Keeping this in mind, you can adapt the game to teach various literacy and numeracy skills. Table 19 shows how the cards may be changed to teach different skills.

TABLE 19. *Variations on the 'Concentration' game*

	SKILL	CARDS
1.	Sentence reading	Ten basic sentences are divided in two parts and written on two different cards, e.g.: I am ... reading. Mother is ... cooking. The farmer is ... sowing seeds.
2.	Vocabulary	Ten sets of cards with words having the same meaning, e.g.: happy ... glad beautiful ... pretty Ten sets of cards with 'opposite' words, e.g.: happy ... sad pretty ... ugly Ten sets of cards with the masculine and feminine form of appropriate words.
3.	Phonics	Ten sets of words having the same vowel sound, e.g.: cat ... map bed ... get
4.	Reading comprehension	Ten cards with questions and ten with the answers. Ten cards with incomplete sentences and ten with suitable words to complete them.
5.	Letter recognition	Ten cards with different lower-case letters and the other ten with corresponding capital letters.
6.	Simple addition	Ten cards with different addition problems (e.g., $3+7=?$) and the other ten with the correct totals.

WHAT'S NEW?

Purpose of the game: To provide practice in sight reading.

Materials: A set of flashcards similar to those used in the 'Concentration' game. There are ten cards with pictures and ten with corresponding words.

Number of players: Three to six.

Approximate time requirement: Fifteen to thirty minutes. The game can be replayed any number of times.

Play:

1. One player is chosen to be the game leader. He spreads all cards face up on the floor. The cards are not arranged in any particular order, but players should be able to see all the pictures and the words clearly.

2. After the players look at the cards and the pictures for about a minute, the leader asks them to close their eyes. He removes one of the picture cards and rearranges the remaining cards in a different order.

3. Players now open their eyes and try to find out which picture card is missing. They can do this from memory or by reading the words to identify the one which does not have a corresponding picture. The first player to pick up the word card for which there is no matching picture card scores a point.

4. The word card is removed and the players close their eyes again. The game leader removes another picture card and rearranges cards. Players open their eyes and try to find the word card for which there is no picture card.

5. This procedure is repeated until there are only five sets of cards (ten cards) on the floor. When the players close their eyes again the game leader *adds* a word card. Players open their eyes and try to locate the word card for which there is no matching picture card as before. This procedure of adding a word card is repeated until the original collection of twenty cards is back on the floor. The player with the highest score wins the game.

Variations:

1. There are ten picture cards showing a farmer doing different things. There are ten corresponding sentence cards describing what is happening in the picture. The game is played as before. Players have to read the entire sentence in order to match it with a picture.

2. There are ten question cards and ten picture cards which give the answers. The object of the game is to find the question for which there is no picture-answer.

3. There are ten cards with simple addition and subtraction problems and ten others with the answers. The player has to find the problem for which there is no answer card.

THREE CARD SETS

Purpose of the game: To provide practice in reading comprehension.

Materials: Flashcards with pictures, words and sentences. For example, if the game is about different farm crops, the picture card shows a sugar cane, the word card says 'sugar cane' and the sentence card says, 'This plant helps us produce sweets'. The sentence card does not use the same word so that the player has to read and understand what it says before he can match it with the word card. About ten sets of these cards (thirty cards in all) are needed for the game.

Number of players: Two to six.

Approximate time requirement: Fifteen to thirty minutes.

Play:

1. The object of the game is to get a set of three cards involving the same object. For example, a set may contain: (a) a card showing a picture of a cotton plant; (b) a card with the word 'cotton'; and (c) a card with the sentence, 'This plant helps us make cloth'.
2. One player shuffles all the cards and gives each player five cards. The remaining cards are placed face down in the middle of the table. The top card of this pile is placed face up beside it.
3. The players take turns to do the following: (a) take either the top card from the face-down pile or the face up card beside it; (b) place this card with the other cards in the hand; and (c) remove any card which is not useful for making a set and place it face up on top of the other face-up cards.
4. Play continues in this fashion until a player has a set of three cards involving the same object. Other players check to make sure that the word and the sentence cards match the picture. If they do, the player wins the game.

Variations:

1. The cards may contain words from different groups such as plants, animals, birds, farm equipment, etc. The object of the game is to collect three cards belonging to the same group.
2. The cards have questions. The object of the game is to find three cards with questions which have the same answer (e.g., 'Which plant has white flowers?', 'Which plant grows twenty-feet tall?', and 'Which plant has a sour fruit?').

3. The cards have pictures. The object of the game is to find a set of three pictures whose names begin with the same sound.

4. The cards have different words. The object of the game is to find three words with similar endings.

5. The cards have addition and subtraction problems. The object of the game is to find three cards which have the same answer (e.g., $2+3=?$, $7-2=?$, and $1+4=?$).

TIC TAC TOE (NOUGHTS AND CROSSES)

FIGURE 37. *Tic tac toe board*

	Select an answer	One-word answer	Long answer
Planting			
Controlling pests			
Harvesting			

Purpose of the game: To provide practice in answering questions at different levels of difficulty.

Materials: A game board as shown in Figure 37. It is in the form of a big square divided into nine smaller squares. Each row stands for a different task. In the example, they represent planting, controlling pests, and harvesting. Each column represents different difficulty levels of questions. The first column is for multiple-choice questions, the second one is for questions which require a single-word answer and the third one is for more difficult questions.

Cards with questions about the three different tasks and at each of the three different levels are also needed for the game. There should be at least five questions for each category. The correct answer to the question is found on the back of the card.

Number of players: Two. If there are more players, the game can be played by two teams of players. Members of each team take turns to answer the questions.

Approximate time requirement: Thirty minutes.

Play:

1. The first player selects one of the small squares on the board. The other player pulls out a suitable question card. For example, the first player wants to play for the middle square. The other player finds a card with a question about controlling pests requiring a one-word answer.

2. The first player now reads the question and chooses the correct answer (if it is a multiple-choice question) or gives an answer. The other player checks it with the answer on the back of the card.

3. If the player's answer is correct, he places one of his pebbles on the appropriate square. If incorrect, he does nothing.

4. The second player now chooses a square he wants to play for. The first player finds him a suitable question card. The game is played as before.

5. The object of the game is to place three pebbles of the same colour in a straight line. They could be horizontal, vertical or diagonal as in these figures:

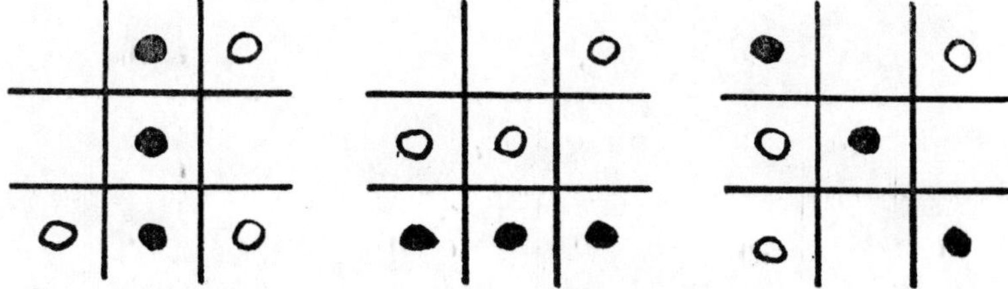

Variations: By changing the content areas represented by the rows, the game can be adapted to review any subject matter.

PRACTICAL EXERCISE

Select one of the sample games described in this chapter on a popular game played in the community. Modify it to teach a suitable literacy skill to your learner. Use the following steps:

1. *Specify the literacy skill to be attained by the players.*
2. *Specify what the players already know.*
3. *Modify the game to teach the literacy skill.*
4. *Prepare game materials (e.g., flashcards, scoring sheets, etc.).*
5. *Write the rules for the game.*
6. *Make changes in the rules to make the game more interesting and effective.*

CHAPTER TEN

Programmed instruction on a large scale

The production of programmes is a time-consuming job which requires the efforts of experts and learners. So much work is involved in the production of even a single programme that, to produce a complete set of materials, you need a large group of people. This chapter is for those higher-level administrators who are able to undertake a major literacy materials project.

Organizing a programmer's workshop

One way of producing a set of programmes is to conduct a workshop for literacy workers. Before conducting the actual workshop, the leader holds a conference to identify a set of subject-matter areas and literacy skills. Literacy workers attending the workshops are then given these topics so that they can produce programmes which are immediately usable in a large-scale literacy project. The workshop also provides time and support for final production and evaluation of the programmes.

Before the workshop: planning conference

When different programmers write individual programmes, they cannot be used as a sequence because no attention is given to the control of the language, vocabulary and the linguistic skills. A pre-workshop conference permits a systematic analysis of major literacy skills. The procedure used in this conference is very similar to the analysis stage of the programming process. Instead of taking a single subject-matter area, breaking it down into learning activities and identifying related literacy skills, this conference takes regional development as the major subject matter and breaks it down into a number of topics. It also identifies the scope and sequence of the literacy skills to accompany these topics. As a result of the conference, a comprehensive syllabus for a literacy programme is drawn up.

In the first phase of the conference, potential learners from the community and various experts identify the developmental goals of the region. During the conference different teams of experts and community members discuss the importance of various topics and identify the most urgent ones. Once the major topics are identified in this way, a group of subject-matter experts can specify the instructional objectives. At the same time, a group of language specialists can work out a set of literacy skills. These two groups can then discuss with each other and develop a general outline for a functional literacy programme.

During the workshop: training and production
The number of participants attending the workshop depends upon the resources and the skills of the workshop leader. Usually between fifteen and thirty participants make up a convenient group.

One of the first activities at the workshop is to divide the participants into teams of three or more to work on the same programme. This team arrangement helps people to learn from each other. Each team begins by selecting a suitable subject matter for the programme. It should be a brief topic to permit rapid production. In the workshop, lectures are kept to a minimum. Literacy workers can learn the skills of programming more effectively through these four methods:

Self instruction on basic principles: Copies of this book and others in the series should be available to all participants prior to the workshop. They will provide a general guideline for programme production. In addition, the workshop leader may prepare some materials on topics of local importance. About an hour each morning is spent on the discussion of the principles and skills covered in a specific chapter of this book. The rest of the day is spent on applying these principles to the production of a programme.

Practical work: The most effective learning takes place when the trainee attempts to apply what he has read in the books to the production of his own programme. This is a major activity in the workshop. Specific times are established for the completion of subject-matter analysis, literacy-skill analysis, an outline for the programme in terms of test frames and the teaching frames. Participants are encouraged to submit their products in time even if they are not completely satisfied.

Imitation: A short sample programme is given to all workshop participants. This contains such intermediate products as subject-matter and literacy-skills analyses and test frames. Participants can use this programme as a model for the one they are to produce.

Team learning: Many steps in the programming process require different people working with each other. Team members can learn from each other, from the members of the community and various experts. Another way to encourage co-operative learning is to spend some time every morning so that the teams can share their problems and solutions. If a team is stopped at a difficult point in the subject-matter analysis, for example, it may discuss this problem with other teams. An opaque projector (epidiascope) is a useful piece of equipment for this type of discussion. If the workshop leader has seen a good piece of work he may request the team to share it with others.

Sequence of workshop activities

The general sequence of the workshop activities is the same as the sequence of the programming process. After each team has chosen its subject matter, its members go through learner analysis, subject-matter analysis, literacy-skills analysis and frame writing. During each of these steps they use the four learning activities of studying books, applying the principles to the design of their own programme, imitating the sample programme, and receiving help from others. A large amount of time is spent on the actual writing of the frames. The workshop then moves into expert evaluation during which experts from outside and the actual participants suggest suitable revisions in different programmes. After these revisions the work-shop leader makes arrangements for the production of multiple copies of each programme. Try-outs are conducted near the workshop. If suitable learners are not available, participants wait until they return to their region. Each participant is asked to test his team's programme and also one from another team. It is a good idea to bring the participants back to the workshop after the try-outs for making final revisions and assembling all programmes.

Ingredients for a productive workshop

A successful workshop needs an effective workshop leader and various materials, equipment and people. The workshop also requires copies of books on programmed instruction and literacy. During the pre-workshop conference and during the analysis and evaluation stages a number of technical experts, language specialists and learners from the community are also needed. Supplies include paper and pens, typewriters, mimeograph or cyclostyle machines, and blackboards. Typists, artists and other technical staff are needed to convert rough copies of the programme into neat and legible versions. The most important ingredient for the success of such a workshop is, of course, a group of enthusiastic participants.

Sample schedule for a workshop

Table 20 indicates a schedule showing approximate time requirements for a programmer-training workshop. Depending upon local needs and conditions, the time allotted for each activity can be increased or reduced.

TABLE 20. *A schedule indicating approximate time requirements for a programmer-training workshop*

ACTIVITY	TIME REQUIRED
Preworkshop conference:	
Meeting to identify priority areas for programme development	1 day
Production of a syllabus for literacy training through programmed instruction	4 days
Workshop:	
Introduction, organization of teams and selection of subject matter	1 day
Learner analysis	1 day
Subject-matter analysis	1 day
Literacy-skills analysis	1 day
Writing frames	5 days
Expert evaluation	2 days
Field testing tryouts	1–2 months
Final revisions and plans for future activities	5 days

After the workshop

A single workshop is seldom sufficient to make an appreciable impression on the problems of literacy. These workshops may be repeated on an annual basis. If the workshop leader takes time to evaluate the programmes and the suggestions from the participants, he will discover a number of ways for making it more effective.

Translating literacy programmes

In a region where there are many different languages, translating a programme from one language to another saves time and effort. It may appear impossible to translate a programme to teach the same literacy skills in another language. For example, translating a programme from English into a regional language changes the level of the language so much that it is impossible to teach the same literacy skills.

However, if we look at the programming process, we can treat translation from a different point of view. In the production of a programme the steps of subject-matter analysis and learner analysis are not affected to a large extent by the language. If we translate an existing programme into another language, we save these steps. The translation does not produce the final version of the programme. It is merely an initial version to be developmentally tested and revised. By using this approach we eventually end up with a revision to teach suitable literacy skills in the second language without having to work through the entire programming process. We are not talking about a literal word-by-word translation of each frame. Instead, the content and the organization of the frames are rewritten in another language with the object of teaching certain specific literacy skills. In this sense, we can even translate a programme from one level of a language to another level of the same language. Let us assume that you have a programme for illiterates and that there is a need for the same programme by another community of neo-literates. You cannot use the programme in its present form because it is too slow for this community. In this case, you 'translate' the programme to a higher literacy level by combining a number of frames and increasing the difficulty level. Through systematic try-outs, you should be able to ensure another highly effective version of the programme.

In conducting a programmer-training workshop you can have different teams working on the same subject matter but in different languages. In a situation like this, Dr. Krishnamurty and I have used a special method for permitting easy translation of programmes. We developed the first version in English which was a common language for both of us. This programme was then translated into each of our languages, Telugu and Tamil. After separate try-outs we classified the types of revisions into subject-matter changes and language changes. Language changes were limited to the appropriate language version. But the subject-matter changes were made in both language versions. When there was a need to translate the programme into another language, the English version served as an effective starting point.

Using programmes

Even the most effective programme is of little value unless it is used in the field. In a large-scale project, it is very important to make careful plans for the wide-spread use of programmes.

Final production

Before the programme is sent to others, it has to be produced in a final form. When field testing shows consistent results, it is time to make plans for this final production. Here are some practical suggestions for this activity:

1. Prepare a suitable acknowledgement page. It is important to remember that the final version of the programme is the collaborative effort of many people. Prepare a page listing the role played by different people. Be sure to include the technical experts, language specialists, and the literacy workers who helped you during the analysis and evaluation stages. The learners who participated in the try-outs also deserve recognition.

2. Obtain copyright for the programme before it is distributed widely. Also obtain permission to reprint any figures, tables and quotations from other books.

3. Identify a suitable publisher for the programme. Usually a literacy agency does not have the resources to publish the programme for mass distribution. You may not find any commercial publisher interested in risking money on your programme. In this case you have to find some funding agency to subsidize the printing.

4. Produce a complete programme. It is important that the programme includes all figures, tables, maps and other elements as well as instructions to the teacher and the user. It is a good idea to bind all these different materials together so that they do not get lost.

Final evaluation

This type of evaluation answers the question: 'Should I use this programme and if I use it, what will it do for the learners?'. Final evaluation provides information to literacy workers and administrators to help them decide whether to use the programme. As Dr. Susan Markle points out, these people need an answer to the question: 'Who learns what, in how much time, under what conditions?'.

Final evaluation is similar to the field testing described in Chapter 6. The main difference is that the information is not used for the improvement of the programme but for describing its effects. Here are some of the major types of information to be collected:

Who learns? We need a complete description of the type of learners. This description should include age, sex, occupation, educational level, language level, and experience. All this information helps a potential user of the programme to compare the level of his learner with the test learners.

What do they learn? A complete description of the objectives of the programme is also included in the final report. In addition, there should be information about the achievement of these objectives. This can be done by providing percentages of learners who answered each test frame correctly.

How much time does it take? This is an important piece of information for planning your schedule. It is important to indicate not only the average time, but also the range of time taken by the slowest to the fastest learner. In addition to providing information on the programme as a whole, you may also report the time required for each unit.

What are the learning conditions? Information on how the programme was used and especially on the role of the teacher should also be provided in the final report. It is important to know whether it assumed the major teaching responsibility. If there were regular classroom meetings, you should also describe what exactly happened during these sessions. Finally, the types of problems reported by learners provide the total picture.

The role of the teacher in programmed instruction

Although programmed instruction is a self-instructional method, many studies indicate that the success of a programme depends upon the way in which the teacher uses it. The skills for using a programme are simple. It is the teacher's attitude toward programmed instruction which is a more critical factor. The typical teacher enjoys his power and authority in the classroom. He plays the role of a wise leader and insists that every student listen attentively to what he says. The value of a teacher is usually measured in terms of how hard he works. The basic philosophy of programmed instruction is directly opposite to this. In programmed instruction, the focus is on learning. It does not matter how hard the teacher works if it produces no learning on the part of the student.

Many teachers do not understand the change in their role in working with programmes. The traditional teacher does not like to give up his authority. He has to be told that programmed instruction merely assumes the responsibilities for some mechanical aspects of teaching. This permits the teacher to do the creative work of inspiring and guiding the learners to become independent readers.

Much of the teacher's function in using programmes involves helping individual learners. With illiterate learners, individual tutoring with programmes is a very effective technique. With learners at an advanced level, the teacher can spend his time more effectively in conducting a 'class'. In this approach each learner obtains social support from his classmates. However, even in this group situation, the teacher is concerned with the needs of individual learners. Here are some practical suggestions for teachers:

1. Before the classes begin, the teacher should become familiar with the programme. The best way to do this is to go through the entire programme, working through each frame, making active responses and comparing them with the correct answers.

2. If the teacher is not familiar with the subject matter of the programme, he should read books dealing with the topic. It is assumed that the teacher is familiar with the literacy skills covered in the programme. If he has any questions about the usage of the language he should consult an expert and clear up his doubts.

3. Even if the learners are to receive instruction on an individual basis, it is a good idea to have the class meet as a group the first time. During this introductory session, the teacher should provide each learner with his own copy of the programme and explain how to use it. The teacher should emphasize that different learners take different times to complete their lessons. He should also inform the learners that the questions in the programme are not to test them but to help them learn better.

4. During the first session, the teacher should explain his role clearly. The responsibility for learning from the programme rests with the learner. However, the teacher is available for help. During later sessions, the teacher works out the exact amount of help to be given to each individual learner. He should try to discourage learners from asking for his help without trying to learn on their own. At the same time, he should also make sure that no learner becomes frustrated through repeated failures.

5. The teacher should begin each class period with a few minutes of general discussion. During this time, he should encourage the learners to talk about the new things they have learned. After this discussion, each learner works through the programme on his own. The teacher moves among the learners to help anyone if needed. He should make it a point to visit each learner at least once. If a learner does not require his help, he should talk with him briefly and praise his efforts.

6. There are two ways for indicating how much work is to be done during each class period. In the first method, the teacher specifies the time period (e.g., thirty minutes) during which all learners work on

their programmes. In the second method, the teacher specifies the number of frames to be finished by each learner. If the time is given to all learners, some will finish more frames than the others. If the same number of frames is required, the faster learners will finish earlier than the slower ones. This makes it possible for the teacher to spend more time with the slower learners. In either method, the teacher should keep daily records of the learner's progress.

7. It is a good idea to change the type of learning activities so that the learners do not become tired of programmed instruction. From time to time the teacher may play a game, show a film, or bring in an expert for a talk.

8. After the first few class sessions, the teacher gets a good idea of what each learner is capable of doing. He may then ask the faster learners to take the programmes home. With the slower learners, the teacher may provide help. Sometimes the faster learners may be asked to tutor the slower ones. In this process, both of them gain many benefits.

Summary

In this chapter we shifted our attention from single programmes to large-scale programming efforts. A workshop on programmed instruction can train literacy workers and also produce sets of programmed materials. There are suitable techniques for translating programmes into different languages. In this chapter a number of suggestions were offered for final production and evaluation. The training of the teacher is an important element in the successful use of any programme. The teacher has to assume a different role to provide the best type of instruction to each and every student.

PRACTICAL EXERCISE

Plan for the following activities related to large-scale use of programmed materials:

1. *A workshop for training literacy workers on preparing programmed materials.*

2. *A workshop for training teachers on the effective use of programmes in literacy training.*

3. *A system for translating a programme from one language into another and for making modifications on the basis of evaluation.*

Glossary of programmed-instruction terms

ADJUNCT PROGRAMME: This type of programme is very similar to a workbook. The learner reads a story and answers a series of questions related to it. Correct answers and references are provided for each question.

ANALYSIS: The planning stage of the *programming process*.[1] During this stage, the programmer studies the learner, the subject matter, and the language for his programme. At the end of this stage, he prepares an outline for the programme.

BEHAVIOURAL OBJECTIVE: This is a statement of the instructional goal in terms of what the learner will be able to do. A behavioural objective includes the learner behaviour, the conditions under which this behaviour is to take place, and the standards for this behaviour.

BRANCHING PROGRAMME: A special type of programme in which the frames are larger than in the linear variety. Each frame contains a *multiple-choice question*. Depending upon the learner's choice of answer, he is sent to different frames. If his choice is incorrect, the next frame explains his error and sends him back for another try.

BRIGHTENING: A prompting procedure frequently used in programmed-tutoring. The tutor presents the question at the most difficult level. If the learner is not able to give the correct answer, the tutor provides more and more *prompts* until he is able to answer correctly.

COMMUNITY: This word is used in a special sense to refer to the group to which the learners belong. Members of this type of community need not live close to each other. For example, 'married women with at least one child' could be the description of a learning community for a *programme* on child care.

COMMUNITY EXPERT: One of the people who evaluate the first version of the programme and suggest ways to make it more suitable for the *community*. A local literacy worker who knows the needs of the people in the community is an example of this type of expert.

COMPLETION QUESTION: A special form of *direct question*. The learner reads an incomplete sentence with a blank. He fills in the blank with the suitable word or words.

CONTENT PROGRAMME: A part of programmed-tutoring materials which contains frames for the learner.

DIRECT QUESTION: A major type of question used in frames. These questions require the learner to write the answer.

EXPERT EVALUATION: One of the steps in the *programming process*. During this step, the first version of the programme is shown to different experts (e.g., a technical expert and a language expert) who make suggestions for

[1]Words in italic are defined in this glossary.

changes. *Revisions* are made on the basis of this evaluation to improve the programme.

FADING: Gradually removing *prompts* so that the learner is able to give the correct answer without them. In the first frame of the series, the strongest prompt is used. In the next frame the prompt is partially removed. This procedure is continued until the prompt is completely removed in the *test frame*.

FIELD TESTING: The final phase of learner try-outs. During this phase the programme is used by a literacy worker under actual field situations. Based on his report, suitable changes are made to improve the programme.

FRAME: A small unit of a *programme*. There are two types of frames: *teaching frames* and *test frames*.

GROUP TESTING: The second phase of learner try-outs. During this phase the programme is used by a small group in an actual classroom situation. The programmer collects information from this group to improve his programme.

INCOMPLETE ANALYSIS: A *subject-matter analysis* in which the *learning activities* do not add up to the *instructional task*. This analysis should be continued further to find out the missing activities.

INDIVIDUAL TESTING: The first phase of learner try-outs. During this phase the programme is presented to one learner at a time by the programmer. The learner's remarks, responses and reactions are used for improving the programme.

INSTRUCTIONAL SEQUENCE: The arrangement of *learning activities* is the order in which they are to be taught in the programme. The instructional sequence forms an outline for the programme.

INSTRUCTIONAL TASK: This is a statement of the selected subject matter for the programme. The instructional task is stated in the form of a *behavioural objective*.

LEARNER ANALYSIS: The first step in the *programming process* during which the programmer studies the needs of the community to which the learners belong. During this step he also finds out how much of the subject matter and literacy skills the learners already know.

LEARNER ACTIVITY: A simpler part of the *instructional task*. Learning activities are identified by repeatedly asking the question, 'What should the learner be able to do in order to perform the instructional task?'. For example, if the instructional task were to cook a soy bean meal, the learning activities will include cleaning the soy beans, boiling the water, cooking the soy beans, adding salt, draining the water and adding spices.

LINEAR PROGRAMME: A self-instructional programme in which all learners go from one frame to the next in the same order. However, each learner works at his own speed.

LITERACY EXPERT: One of the people who evaluates the first version of the programme and suggests ways to improve the language. A linguist or a language teacher may play the role of this expert.

LITERACY-SKILLS ANALYSIS: One of the steps of the *programming process* in which the *programmer* studies the language required for teaching the selected subject matter. During this analysis he prepares a list of words, sentences and other language elements to be taught in the programme.

MATCHING QUESTION: A special form of *selection question*. The learner studies two columns of related sentences or phrases. He connects matching phrases by drawing a line.

MEDIA PROGRAMME: A special type of programme using a combination of one or more media such as filmstrip, television, tape recording, and radio broadcast.

MULTIPLE-CHOICE QUESTION: A special form of *selection question*. The learner reads a question which is followed by a number of possible answers. He chooses the best answer among them.

MULTIPLE-TRACK PROGRAMME: A special type of *linear programme* in which each frame is provided in two different versions. The top frame on each page provides the fast track. It uses a higher level of language and asks a difficult question. If the learner finds it too hard, he may drop down to a set of easier frames dealing with the same subject matter.

OPERATIONAL PROGRAMME: A part of programme-tutoring materials which tells the tutor what to do. The operational programme gives different steps in the tutoring procedure and provides instructions for different types of answers from the learner.

PRINCIPLES OF PROGRAMMED INSTRUCTION: Basic ideas from psychology and good teaching practice which are applied to make a *programme* effective. Among these principles are the following: (a) learning should take place in small steps; (b) the learner should learn actively; (c) the learner should check his answers immediately; (d) learning should be from the simple to the complex; (e) the learner should learn at his own speed.

PROGRAMME: A type of instructional material which is organized in a special way. The lesson in a programme is divided into small units called *frames*. *Teaching frames* give new information, ask questions and give the correct answers. *Test frames* ask questions about the previous teaching frames. The learner reads each frame, answers the question and checks his answer. He repeats this procedure until he completes the programme.

PROGRAMMED GAMES: Programmed games are prepared by applying the principles of programmed instruction to learning games. These games provide many practice opportunities to the learner and do not require the presence of the teacher.

PROGRAMMED-TUTORING: Programmed-tutoring materials are prepared by applying the *principles of programmed instruction* to a tutoring situation. The frames of the programme are presented to the learner by a tutor. Depending upon the learner's response, the tutor follows different sets of instruction.

PROGRAMMER: The person who plans and prepares a *programme*, using the *programming process*.

PROGRAMMING PROCESS: The systematic procedure used for preparing *programmes*. The three major steps of the process are *analysis, writing* and *revision*.

PROGRESS SHEET: A part of programmed-tutoring materials. The tutor fills out this sheet during the lesson to show which frames the learner has answered correctly and which ones he missed.

PROMPT: A clue or hint to help the learner give the correct answer. Pictures, underlined words, arrows and parts of the correct word are all examples of prompts.

QUESTIONNAIRE: A set of questions on a common topic used for collecting information on such things as the needs of the *community* or what the learners already know. Questionnaires are directly used with experts, with members of an illiterate or semi-literate community. The programmer uses them as a suggested set of oral questions in an interview situation.

REVISION: Making changes in the *programme* to improve it. This is the last stage of the *programming process*. Revisions are made on the basis of the opinions of experts and the actual results from learners.

SELECTION QUESTION: A major type of question used in *frames*. The learner does not have to write an answer. Instead he merely chooses the correct answer from a list of alternatives.

SEQUENCING QUESTION: A special form of *selection question*. The learner reads a number of sentences which are given in an incorrect order and arranges them in the correct order.

SUBJECT-MATTER ANALYSIS: The second step of the *programming process*. During this step the *programmer* divides the subject matter for his programme into a number of small learning activities. On the basis of this analysis, he prepares an outline for the programme.

SUBJECT-MATTER EXPERT: One of the people who evaluates the first version of the programme and suggests ways to improve it. This person is an expert in the subject matter area covered in the programme. For example, if the programme deals with the use of fertilizers, the local agricultural officer may become the subject-matter expert.

TEACHING FRAME: A small unit of a *programme* which gives some new information. These frames also contain a question to make sure that the learner is learning actively. After giving his answer, the learner checks it with the correct answer given in the frame.

TEST FRAME: A small unit of a programme which tests the learner's understanding of the previous *teaching frames*. The test frame contains a question and the correct answer.

TRUE-FALSE QUESTION: A special form of *selection question*. The learner reads a number of statements and decides which ones are true and which are false.

TRY-OUT: One of the steps of the *programming process* during which the *programmer* tries out the *programme* on a learner. The purpose of this step is not to test the learner but to find out how the programme can be improved. On the basis of the errors made by the learner, the programme is revised.

WASH-AHEAD PROGRAMME: A special type of *linear programme* in which the first frame is a *test frame*. If the learner answers the question correctly, he is asked to skip a set of *teaching frames* and go directly to the next unit.

WASH-BACK PROGRAMME: A special type of *linear programme* in which the *test frames* tell the learner to return to previous frames if he makes an error. The learner is required to study these frames and answer the test frame again.

WRITING: The middle stage of the *programming process*. During this stage, the *programmer* uses the outline from the *analysis* stage. In writing the programme, he uses the *principles of programmed instruction*.